READING
Grade 2

Table of Contents

Credits:
McGraw-Hill Children's Publishing Editorial/Production Team
Vincent F. Douglas, B.S. and M. Ed.
Tracey E. Dils
Jennifer Blashkiw Pawley
Teresa A. Domnauer
Tracy R. Paulus
Suzanne M. Diehm

Big Tuna Trading Company Art/Editorial/Production Team
Mercer Mayer
John R. Sansevere
Erica Farber
Brian MacMullen
Matthew Rossetti
Billy Steers
Diane Dubreuil
Atomic Age, Inc.

McGraw-Hill
Children's Publishing

A Division of The McGraw-Hill Companies

Text Copyright © 2001 McGraw-Hill Children's Publishing.
Art Copyright © 2001 Mercer Mayer.

Send all inquiries to: McGraw-Hill Children's Publishing, 8787 Orion Place, Columbus OH 43240-4027

1-57768-812-0

4 5 6 7 8 9 10   VHG   06 05 04 03 02

Trouble with Blue

Read to see why Little Critter has to clean up the garden.

1   Little Critter saw his mom standing at the door of his room. "Mom, why are you holding a shovel?" asked Little Critter.

2   "I think you will need it, Little Critter," said Mrs. Critter.

3   "Why?" asked Little Critter.

4   "Come downstairs and see," said Little Sister, poking her head inside.

5   Little Critter followed his mom and sister out to the yard. The garden was a mess!

6   "Oh, no!" said Little Critter. "Blue's been digging again."

7   "Little Critter," said Mrs. Critter, "I think Blue needs to be trained."

8   "You're right, Mom," agreed Little Critter. "I better train him. It shouldn't be hard. Blue is smart."

9   Blue barked and wagged his tail. Little Sister giggled as she looked at Blue's muddy paws. "He doesn't look very smart to me!"

4

Knowing the Words

Write the story words that have these meanings.

1. a tool that scoops

   _____
   (Par. 1)

2. place where plants grow

   _____
   (Par. 5)

3. taught

   _____
   (Par. 7)

Reading and Thinking

1. This story is mostly about

   _____ Little Critter's room.

   _____ a problem with Blue.

   _____ a problem with Little Sister.

Words such as **he, she**, and **it** take the place of other words. Read these sentences. Then fill in the blanks.

Little Critter shouted as he ran.
He stands for _Little Critter_.

2. Her mom laughed as she talked.

   She stands for _____.

3. My dad talked as he worked.

   He stands for _____.

A Talk with Blue

Read to see what Little Critter tells Blue.

1 Little Critter and Little Sister helped their mom all afternoon. They filled the holes that Blue had dug. They planted new flowers. Little Critter tried to water the garden, but Blue wanted to play.

2 "Get out of the way, Blue!" yelled Little Critter.

3 Blue didn't listen. He just barked and shook himself. Water flew everywhere, getting Mom and Little Sister both very wet. They went inside to dry off.

4 Little Critter shook his head. "Blue, we need to talk," he said. He climbed into Blue's doghouse. Blue climbed in after him. "Blue, you have to stop digging," said Little Critter. "And you have to learn how to listen. I don't want you to get into more trouble. You're a smart dog. I just know you can be good."

5 Little Critter hugged his dog. Blue gave Little Critter a big, wet kiss.

6 "I hope that means yes," said Little Critter.

Reading and Thinking

Put each word in the right blank.

dig   garden   inside

1. Little Critter helped fix the _____.

2. Blue likes to _____.

3. Little Critter sat _____ the doghouse.

Circle the right answer.

4. What does Little Critter want Blue to do?
   stay in the doghouse
   stop digging
   water the garden

5. What did Little Critter tell Blue?

   _____

   _____

Working with Words

Circle the best word for each sentence. Then write it in the blank.

1. Little Critter and Blue _____ in the doghouse.
   sat   can   cat

2. Blue likes to _____ in the garden.
   dog   dig   dug

3. Little Critter will _____ Blue.
   trap   rain   train

Blue Gets Out

Read to find out where Blue goes.

1 The next day, Little Critter's mom asked him to get the mail.

2 "Sure, Mom," answered Little Critter. He walked down the path to the mailbox. He unlatched the gate, opened the mailbox, and got the mail. On his way back to the house, he looked at the mail.

3 Just then Blue saw the open gate. He dashed past Little Critter and ran out of the yard. "Blue, come back!" cried Little Critter. "Here, Blue!" Little Critter dropped the mail and chased his dog.

4 Blue jumped over a fence. Little Critter jumped over the fence. Blue crawled under some bushes. Little Critter crawled under the bushes. He could not catch Blue. Little Critter ran through his neighbors' yards and called for Blue. He ran right into Mrs. Crabtree.

5 "I'm sorry, Mrs. Crabtree. I was just looking for..." Little Critter tried to explain.

6 Mrs. Crabtree frowned. "I think I know just who you are looking for," she said.

8

Knowing the Words

Write the story words that have these meanings.

1. place for mail

_____
(Par. 2)

2. ran after

_____
(Par. 3)

3. made an unhappy face

_____
(Par. 6)

Reading and Thinking

1. What is the name of Little Critter's neighbor?

_____

Why do you think she was frowning?

_____

_____

2. What happened first in the story? Put **1** by it. What happened next? Put **2** by it. Put **3** by the thing that happened last.

_____ Little Critter chased Blue.

_____ Little Critter ran into Mrs. Crabtree.

_____ Little Critter went to get the mail.

Mrs. Crabtree's Roses

Read to see why Little Critter has to check his piggy bank.

1 "Your dog has dug up my prize-winning roses," said Mrs. Crabtree. She pointed to her yard. There were pink and red flowers everywhere.

2 "I'm really sorry, Mrs. Crabtree," said Little Critter. "Blue just likes to dig. Don't worry. I promise it won't happen again." Blue lay down at Little Critter's feet and put his head on the ground. "See, Mrs. Crabtree. Blue is sorry, too," added Little Critter.

3 "Those roses were my pride and joy," said Mrs. Crabtree. "You will have to pay for them. I think twenty dollars is about right."

4 "Okay, Mrs. Crabtree," said Little Critter. "I'll pay you back as soon as I can."

5 Little Critter walked slowly home with Blue.

6 "Blue, this is just the kind of trouble I was talking about," said Little Critter. "Twenty dollars is a lot of money. I better go check my piggy bank."

Reading and Thinking

1. What did Blue do? _____
   _____

2. How did Blue show he was sorry?
   _____
   _____

3. Why did Little Critter want to check
   his piggy bank? _____
   _____

Working with Words

Circle the best word for each sentence. Then write it in the blank.

1. Little Critter will _____ for the roses.

   day   say   pay

2. _____ you for the new toy.

   Bank   Thank   Think

3. Blue put his head on the _____.

   grow   grind   ground

4. Little Critter walked _____ with Blue.

   hope   hum   home

Little Critter's Friends Help Out

Read to find out how Little Critter's friends try to help.

1   The next day, Little Critter was playing with his friends, Maurice, Molly, Gabby, and Tiger. He told them all about Blue and Mrs. Crabtree's roses. He told them about the twenty dollars.

2   "Boy, was she mad," said Little Critter. "And I only have $2.23 in my piggy bank. Mom says I have to earn the rest."

3   "I have a dollar you can have," said Tiger. He pulled a crumpled dollar bill from his pocket.

4   "You can have my allowance," added Gabby. "I was only going to buy candy anyway." Gabby handed Little Critter some coins.

5   "We can help, too," said the twins, Maurice and Molly, at the same time.

6   "Thanks a lot," said Little Critter. "I bet this will be enough."

7   Little Critter counted the money. It came to $5.27.

8   "You need lots more than that," said Gabby. "But don't worry. I think I know just how we can earn the rest."

Knowing the Words

Write the story words that have these meanings.

1. people you like a lot

   _____
   (Par. 1)

2. crushed or wrinkled

   _____
   (Par. 3)

Circle the three words in each line that belong together.

3. house   book   park   store

4. bark   fly   howl   jump

5. soup   lunch   dinner   breakfast

6. ball   friend   neighbor   aunt

Reading and Thinking

1. This story is mostly about

   _____ how Blue caused trouble.

   _____ how Little Critter's friends help.

   _____ how Blue earns money.

2. Why does Little Critter need more money?

   _____

   _____

3. Can you think of a way for Little Critter to earn money?

   _____

   _____

Gabby's Idea

Read to see what the friends plan.

1   A little while later, Gabby came over to Little Critter's house with a big sign. It read: Lemonade — five cents a cup.

2   "My idea is to open a lemonade stand," said Gabby. "Then we can sell lemonade to make money."

3   "Great idea," said Little Critter. "I'll make the lemonade."

4   "Maurice and I will get paper cups," said Molly.

5   "I'll bring a table and chairs," added Tiger.

6   "Meet you here in half an hour," said Gabby.

7   Little Critter hurried to make the lemonade. The directions said to use two scoops of lemonade mix, but Little Critter used four. He wanted to make sure it tasted really good.

8   Little Critter carried the heavy pitcher outside. "We're ready for business!" he said.

Some of these sentences are about **real** things, things that could happen. Write **R** by them. The other sentences are about things that could not happen, **make-believe** things. Write **M** by them.

1. _____ A dog can run and play.

2. _____ A house can talk.

3. _____ A dog likes bones.

4. _____ A dog likes to read.

5. What was Gabby's idea? _____

_____

Write each set of words in A-B-C order.

1. cups   table   lemonade

_____

_____

_____

2. chairs   idea   house

_____

_____

_____

3. later   sign   money

_____

_____

_____

More Trouble for Blue

Read to see what happens at the lemonade stand.

1 Little Critter and his friends sat at the lemonade stand. Blue lay on the ground at Little Critter's feet and chewed on Little Critter's shoelaces.

2 Just then Su Su walked by with her dog, Fifi. Fifi had pink ribbons in her curly white fur. She smelled like perfume.

3 "Do you want some lemonade, Su Su?" asked Little Critter. "It's only five cents a cup."

4 "Okay," said Su Su. Suddenly, Blue bounded over to Fifi and began to sniff her. The two dogs started to play. Blue ran to the garden and began to dig. Fifi pulled on her leash, trying to follow him.

5 "Stop that right now, Fifi!" ordered Su Su. Fifi wouldn't listen. She pulled so hard, Su Su lost hold of the leash. Fifi ran after Blue.

6 "Here, Fifi!" cried Su Su.

7 "Here, Blue!" called Little Critter. The dogs wouldn't listen. They just kept playing in the dirt.

8 "Fifi is a purebred poodle," Su Su yelled at Little Critter. "And I'm training her for the dog show. I knew I shouldn't let her play with a mutt, like your dog."

9 Su Su stomped off and dragged Fifi out of the dirt. Her ribbons had come untied. Her white fur was all brown.

10 "Oh, no, Blue," said Little Critter. "More trouble."

Reading and Thinking

Put each word in the right blank.

walked   pulled   sniffed

1. Blue _____ Fifi.

2. Su Su _____ with Fifi.

3. Fifi _____ on the leash.

Write **R** by the sentences that are about **real** things. Write **M** by the sentences about **make believe** things.

4. _____ Dogs can make lemonade.

5. _____ People can make lemonade.

6. _____ People put ice in lemonade.

7. _____ Ice keeps drinks warm.

Working with Words

A **base** word is a word without an ending. The words in each row have the same **base** word. Circle the ending of each one. Then write the **base** word in the blank.

1. playing   2. starting
   played   started
   plays   starts

_____   _____

Circle the best word for each sentence. Then write it in the blank.

3. We'll eat _____ he comes.
    then   when   check

4. Please finish _____ apples.
    chase   those   shoes

A Sale

Read to see who is the first customer at the lemonade stand.

1   Little Sister came outside to see how business was going. She laughed when she saw muddy Blue licking the dirt off his paws. "That dog is a mess," said Little Sister. "Have you sold any lemonade yet?"

2   "No," said Little Critter.

3   "Too bad," said Little Sister. "I bet it'll take you forever to make twenty dollars."

4   Just then Mrs. Smith, the letter carrier, came walking toward them. "Lemonade sounds great on this hot day," said Mrs. Smith. "I'll take two cups, please."

5   "See," said Little Critter. He proudly poured two cups.

6   "You're our first customer," added Gabby.

7   Mrs. Smith gave Little Critter two nickels. Then she took a sip of lemonade. She puckered her lips.

8   "How's the lemonade?" asked Little Sister.

9   "Very—um—tasty," said Mrs. Smith.

10   Tiger put the nickels in a cup. He shook the cup. The nickels jingled.

11   "We'll have the twenty dollars in no time," said Little Critter.

Reading and Thinking

1. What did Mrs. Smith say about the lemonade? _____
_____

2. Why was Little Critter proud?
_____
_____

3. Write **1**, **2**, and **3** by these sentences to show what happened first, next, and last.

_____ Mrs. Smith bought lemonade.

_____ Little Sister came outside.

_____ Tiger put the nickels in the cup.

Learning to Study

Write each set of words in A-B-C order.

1.   that   day   outside

_____
_____
_____

2.   nickels   customer   jingled

_____
_____
_____

3.   tasty   muddy   dollars

_____
_____
_____

A Long Way to Twenty Dollars

Read to see how much money Little Critter makes at the lemonade stand.

1 Little Critter and his friends worked at the lemonade stand all afternoon. Mr. and Mrs. Critter each bought a cup of lemonade.

2 "Very tangy, Little Critter," said Mr. Critter.

3 After that, Tiger's brother bought a cup. Maurice and Molly's cousins bought three cups. Gabby's dad bought a cup, too.

4 "Let's count the money," said Little Critter. He and Tiger counted all the coins in the cup. The total only came to forty-five cents.

5 "That's a long way from twenty dollars," said Little Sister. "Maybe you should raise the price."

6 "We just have to be patient," said Little Critter. "I'm sure we'll sell lots more lemonade."

7 At sunset, they had only sold two more cups. Little Critter and his friends were hot and tired.

8 "Don't worry, Little Critter," said Gabby. "We'll think of something."

9 "Maybe we should go into town tomorrow," said Tiger. "I bet we'll find a way to make money there."

10 Little Critter smiled and thanked his friends. "See you tomorrow," he said.

Knowing the Words

Write the story words that have these meanings.

1. paid money for

_____
(Par. 1)

2. make higher

_____
(Par. 5)

3. the next day

_____
(Par. 9)

Put a check by the meaning that fits the underlined word in each sentence.

4. Is it <u>hard</u> to make new friends?

_____ something not soft

_____ something not easy to do

5. I will <u>watch</u> Blue play.

_____ thing that tells time

_____ look at

Reading and Thinking

1. How much money was in the cup?

_____

2. This story is mostly about

_____ why Little Critter needs money.

_____ selling a lot of lemonade.

_____ a slow day at the lemonade stand.

3. Why did Little Sister say to raise the price?_____

_____

4. What did Tiger say to do?

_____

_____

Gabby's New Idea

Read to find out about Gabby's new plan for Blue.

1   The next day, Little Critter and his friends went into town. Little Sister and Blue came, too. Along the way, they passed a notice for the dog show.

2   "I know!" exclaimed Gabby. "Let's enter Blue in the dog show. First prize is twenty-five dollars!"

3   "I don't know, Gabby," said Little Critter. "Blue needs a lot of training."

4   "Don't worry," said Gabby. "I have a book about training dogs."

5   Little Sister giggled. "I hope it's a really good book," she said.

6   "Blue can do it," said Tiger.

7   "No problem," agreed Maurice and Molly.

8   "Dog training will start this afternoon," said Gabby. "We'll work really hard with Blue every day. You'll see. He'll be just as well-behaved as Fifi in no time!"

9   "Woof! Woof!" barked Blue.

Reading and Thinking

1. This story is mostly about

_____ Gabby's idea.

_____ Gabby's dog.

_____ Blue's paws.

2. Gabby wants to train Blue for the show because _____

_____.

3. Do you think that Gabby can train Blue? _____

Working with Words

Circle the best word for each sentence. Then write it in the blank.

1. I want to read this _____.
boat   back   book

2. We will _____ hard.
work   walk   week

Write **-ing** or **-ed** in each blank.

3. I talk _____ with her yesterday.

4. She want _____ to work.

5. Now she is train _____ Blue.

Circle the right word for each sentence. Then write it in the blank.

6. Tiger is my best _____.
ground   proud   friend

7. I need a _____ of water.
trick   drink   break

Little Critter's News

Read to find out if Little Critter's mom and dad like the news.

1 Little Critter ran home with Little Sister and Blue. "Mom! Dad!" he called, as he opened the door. "Guess what? We're going to enter Blue in the dog show! First prize is twenty-five dollars. If Blue wins, then I can pay Mrs. Crabtree the money I owe her."

2 "Good idea," said Mr. Critter. Mrs. Critter thought so, too.

3 Little Sister shook her head. "How are you going to train him if he never listens?" she asked.

4 "Learning to listen is part of the training, Little Sister," said Mrs. Critter. "We have to remember Blue is just a puppy. He can learn."

5 Suddenly, Blue started whining. The Critters saw a puddle on the floor right next to him.

6 "Little Critter, I think Blue needs to go out," said Mr. Critter.

7 "He sure has a lot to learn," said Little Sister.

24

Reading and Thinking

Look at each picture and circle the sentence that goes with it.

1. Blue is playing outside.

   Blue is playing in the house.

2. Blue sleeps on Little Critter's bed.

   Blue sleeps in his doghouse.

3. What did Mr. Critter say about the dog show? _____

   _____

4. What will Little Critter do if Blue wins the dog show? _____

   _____

5. What did Little Sister say about Blue? _____

   _____

Working with Words

Circle the best word for each sentence. Then write it in the blank.

1. Blue has a _____.

   tan   than   tail

2. Blue can win a _____.

   prize   quiet   paint

3. The floor was_____.

   pet   met   wet

Write these sentences. Use one of the shorter words from the box to stand for the words that are underlined.

| We'll | isn't | can't | didn't | I'm |

4. We will be there.

   _____

5. He did not go.

   _____

6. The puppy is not hurt.

   _____

7. I am hungry.

   _____

8. Blue cannot do tricks.

   _____

Blue's First Lesson

Read to see how much Blue has to learn.

1 Gabby, Maurice, Molly, and Tiger all came over to Little Critter's house to help train Blue. Gabby brought her dog training book, *Dog Training the Easy Way*.

2 "I don't think there is an easy way to train Blue," said Little Sister. Maurice and Molly laughed.

3 "Lesson One: Teach Your Dog His Name," Gabby read aloud. "Always use your dog's name when you ask him to do something."

4 "Here, Blue!" Gabby called. Blue jumped up and licked Gabby's face. "You try, Little Critter," she said, as she wiped her face.

5 "Here, Blue!" said Little Critter. Blue jumped on Little Critter and knocked him down. "You try, Tiger," he said.

6 "Here, Blue!" shouted Tiger. Blue bounded toward him and grabbed the baseball out of his hand. Then he ran for the garden with the ball in his mouth.

7 "We're finished with Lesson One," said Gabby. "Blue definitely knows his name."

8 "That's about all he knows," said Little Sister.

1. This story is mostly about

_____ Tiger's ball.

_____ Gabby's dog.

_____ Blue's first lesson.

Fill in the blanks.

2. Little Critter said, "good dog," as he petted Blue.

He stands for _____.

3. Gabby brought her book and put it on the table.

It stands for _____.

Circle the best word for each sentence. Then write it in the blank.

1. The lesson is too _____.

      leg   long   log

2. The dog's eyes are _____.

      big   bag   buy

3. Gabby told Blue to _____.

      sat   set   sit

4. They have a _____ pet.

      now   not   new

Read these words and look at the pictures.

Gabby's friend   her friend's hand

You can see that you add **'s** when you want to show that the hand belongs to Little Critter. Now write these names the same way.

5. Little Critter _____ hand

6. Gabby _____ hand

Too Much Food

Read to see why Blue has a big belly.

1 One morning, Little Sister woke up Little Critter. "You better come see what your dog did," she said.

2 Little Critter followed Little Sister to the kitchen. There was dog food everywhere. Blue had torn open the bag and helped himself.

3 "Blue, you've eaten way too much," said Little Critter. "You don't look good."

4 Just then, there was a knock at the door. It was Gabby. "Hi, Little Critter. Are you ready for the next dog training lesson?" she asked.

5 "He's ready," said Little Sister. "But Blue's not." She pointed to Blue. He was lying on the floor with his stomach sticking out.

6 "He ate too much," said Little Critter. "Now he's so full he can't move."

7 "We'll have the next lesson when Blue feels better," said Gabby.

8 "I hope he's better before the dog show," said Little Critter.

9 "Maybe he could win the prize for the biggest belly!" said Little Sister.

Knowing the Words

Write the story words that have these meanings.

1. ripped _____
   (Par. 2)

2. tapping sound _____
   (Par. 4)

3. set to go _____
   (Par. 4)

Circle the three words in each line that belong together.

4. arms   flowers   feet   hands

5. eyes   ears   bag   mouth

6. hair   brown   white   black

Reading and Thinking

1. This story is mostly about
   _____ the next dog lesson.

   _____ Blue eating too much.

   _____ a new kind of dog food.

2. How do you think Blue feels?

   _____

   _____

3. What do you think Little Critter can do so this won't happen again ?

   _____

Walking on a Leash

Read to see what Blue does at his next lesson.

1 "Now that Blue feels better, he can learn to walk on a leash," said Gabby.

2 Little Critter and his friends went to the Critterville Park. Little Sister came, too.

3 "Lesson Two: Walking on a Leash," Gabby read aloud from her book. "Use the word 'heel' to tell your dog to walk beside you."

4 "Heel, Blue," said Little Critter. Blue wanted to play with the leash instead. He walked around Little Critter.

5 "Heel, Blue," tried Tiger, walking over to Little Critter.

6 "Stop, Tiger," said Gabby. "Only Little Critter should give Blue commands."

7 But it was too late. Blue ran toward Tiger, tangling the leash around Little Critter. Little Critter tripped and fell onto the grass. He knocked into Tiger. Tiger fell on top of Little Critter. Blue stood on top of Tiger and barked.

8 Maurice, Molly, and Little Sister laughed. They helped Little Critter and Tiger to their feet.

9 "Some dogs may need more practice than others," Gabby read.

10 Little Sister giggled. "I think Blue is one of those dogs!"

Reading and Thinking

Put each word in the right blank.

read   learn   better

1. Blue felt much _____.

2. Blue will _____.

3. Gabby _____ her book.

4. Write **1**, **2**, and **3** by these
   sentences to show what happened
   first, next, and last.

   _____ The friends went to the park.

   _____ Little Critter got tangled up.

   _____ Blue wanted to play.

Working with Words

Circle the best word for each sentence.
Then write it in the blank.

1. Can you read this _____?

   cook   look   book

2. Gabby _____ Little Critter today.

   mail   met   mean

3. Blue wanted to _____on
   his bone.

   shoe   chew   threw

The missing word in each sentence
sounds like **right**. Change the **r** in
right to **f**, **l**, or **n**. Write the new
words. The first one is done.

4. _fight_   _____   _____

Use the words you made in sentences.

5. Please turn off the _____.

6. We will not _____ over
   the toys.

7. It rained last _____.

The Missing Slipper

Read to find out what happened to Mr. Critter's slipper.

1 "Little Critter," called Mr. Critter. "Have you seen my other slipper?"

2 Little Critter helped his dad look for the slipper. First, Little Critter looked in his toy box. Then he looked in the kitchen cupboards. He looked under the sofa. He looked in Little Sister's closet. He could not find the slipper anywhere.

3 "Did you check the doghouse?" whispered Little Sister.

4 Little Critter hoped Blue didn't have the slipper. He stuck his head in the doghouse. There was Blue, chewing on Mr. Critter's slipper.

5 "Bad dog," said Little Critter. He took the slipper from Blue. Maybe his dad wouldn't notice.

6 "Dad! Dad!" called Little Critter. "I found your slipper."

7 "Great," said his dad until he saw his slipper. It was soggy and it had holes in it. "It looks like Blue ate my slipper for breakfast," said Mr. Critter.

8 "Sorry, Dad," said Little Critter.

9 Little Sister laughed. "I wonder if Lesson Three will teach Blue not to eat slippers!"

Knowing the Words

Write the story words that have these meanings.

1. soft shoe

_____

(Par. 1)

2. place to keep clothes

_____

(Par. 2)

Circle the three words in each line that belong together.

3. walk   look   trot   run

4. head   tail   trick   feet

5. good   mean   great   wonderful

Reading and Thinking

1. This story is mostly about

_____ the missing slipper.

_____ Blue's doghouse.

_____ breakfast.

2. List three places Little Critter looked for the slipper.

_____

_____

_____

_____

3. Where did Little Critter find the slipper? _____

_____

4. What did Blue do to the slipper?

_____

33

Mrs. Crabtree Stops By

Read to find out what Mrs. Crabtree has to say about the dog show.

1 Gabby came to train Blue every afternoon. No matter how hard Little Critter and his friends worked, Blue still did not listen.

2 One afternoon, when Little Critter was working with Blue, Mrs. Crabtree came over. "Sit, Blue!" said Little Critter. Blue kept rolling around in the grass instead.

3 "Hello!" said Mrs. Crabtree. She looked at Little Critter, then at Blue, and back again. "What are you kids up to?"

4 "Hi, Mrs. Crabtree," said Little Critter. "We're training Blue for the dog show. First prize is twenty-five dollars. If Blue wins, then I can pay you for the roses."

5 "Really?" asked Mrs. Crabtree, looking down at Blue. He was digging a hole at her feet.

6 Little Critter smiled at Mrs. Crabtree. He put his arms around Blue.

7 "Good luck!" said Mrs. Crabtree, frowning.

8 "Good luck!" repeated Little Sister. "You're definitely going to need it!"

Reading and Thinking

1. This story is mostly about

_____ Mrs. Crabtree's roses.

_____ Mrs. Crabtree's visit.

_____ Mrs. Crabtree's feet.

2. Instead of sitting, Blue _____

_____

3. Why do you think Mrs. Crabtree

came over? _____

Working with Words

Circle the best word for each sentence. Then write it in the blank.

1. Mrs. Crabtree _____ over.

stayed   came   ate

2. I see you _____ every day.

her   help   here

3. I _____ to brush my dog.

little   like   let

Read these words and look at the pictures.

dog   dogs

You can see that you add **s** to show that you mean more than one dog. Write these words so that they mean more than one.

4. rose _____

5. friend _____

6. lesson _____

Fifi Shows Off

Read to see why Blue howls at Fifi.

1   Another afternoon during dog training, Su Su walked by with Fifi. Fifi was wearing a sparkly new collar and a pink sweater.

2   "Guess what?" said Gabby. "We're training Blue to enter the dog show, too."

3   "Well, you'll never win," said Su Su. "Fifi is the smartest dog in Critterville. She knows lots of tricks. Watch this." Su Su turned to Fifi. "Sit, Fifi," said Su Su. Fifi sat. "Stay, Fifi," said Su Su. Fifi stayed. "Roll over, Fifi," said Su Su. Fifi rolled over. "Speak, Fifi," said Su Su. Fifi began to yap.

Blue did not like the sound. He began to howl. Fifi started howling, too.

4   Little Critter and Gabby laughed. Tiger howled along with Blue and Fifi. Maurice and Molly clapped for the dogs' song. Su Su covered her ears. "Let's go, Fifi," said Su Su, "before you learn any more bad habits."

5   "Let's try that again," said Gabby. "Sing, Blue!" Blue howled.

6   "Good dog, Blue!" said Little Critter.

7   "At least he knows one trick," said Little Sister.

Put each word in the right blank.

howl   smart   clapped

1. Fifi is so _____.

2. Blue began to _____.

3. Maurice and Molly _____.

4. What was Fifi wearing?

_____

_____

5. How do you know Su Su didn't like the howling sound?

_____

_____

6. This story is mostly about

_____ Fifi's new collar.

_____ Fifi and Blue's trick.

_____ Little Sister's trick.

Write each set of words in A-B-C order.

1.   pink   sing   howl

_____

_____

_____

2.   stay   ears   yap

_____

_____

_____

3.   collar   trick   one

_____

_____

_____

Dizzy Blue

Read to see what all the noise is about.

1 "How are the dog lessons going?" asked Mr. Critter at dinner that night.

2 "Great," said Little Critter. "Blue is really learning to behave."

3 Suddenly, the family heard crashing sounds. They headed for the living room. A chair was lying in the middle of the floor. Next to it was Blue, spinning round and round, chasing his tail.

4 "Stop, Blue!" cried Little Critter.

5 Blue kept spinning. He knocked over a lamp. The lamp knocked some books off the bookcase. The books fell on the table. The table crashed to the floor. Mrs. Critter covered her eyes. Mr. Critter put his arms around Blue. Finally, Blue stopped spinning. He looked very dizzy. He wobbled from side to side.

6 "Easy, Blue!" said Mr. Critter.

7 Little Sister helped Little Critter clean up the mess. It took them so long, Little Critter missed *Super Critter*, his favorite TV show.

8 "Stop looking so mad," said Little Sister. "Blue will learn — someday."

Reading and Thinking

Put each word in the right blank.

Suddenly   bumped   wobbled

1. Blue _____ from side to side.

2. _____, the family heard a crash.

3. Blue _____ into the chair.

4. Why do you think Blue was chasing his own tail? _____

Working with Words

Circle the best word for each sentence. Then write it in the blank.

1. Blue has a _____ tail.

    log   lost   long

2. We will _____ a walk.

    talk   take   tail

The missing word in each sentence sounds like **make**. Change the **m** in **make** to **b, t,** or **w.** Write the new words.

3. _____ _____ _____

Use the words you made in sentences.

4. May we _____ a walk?

5. I like to _____ cookies.

6. Did Blue _____ you?

You know that **Mom's hand** means "the hand of Mom." Add **'s** when you write these names to show what belongs to each.

7. Dad _____ coat

8. Tiger _____ baseball

9. Blue _____ teeth

Little Critter Has the Blues

Read to see how Little Critter's mom helps.

1 Little Critter walked slowly up the stairs to his bedroom. He threw the door open with a bang. He grumbled as he put on his pajamas. Then he got into bed and pulled the covers over his head.

2 "Little Critter," said his mother quietly. "Is everything okay?"

3 "No," said Little Critter. His voice sounded funny from under the covers.

4 "What's wrong?" asked Mrs. Critter.

5 Little Critter pulled down the covers. "Blue is never going to act right," said Little Critter. "He's never going to win the dog show. I'll never be able to pay for Mrs. Crabtree's roses."

6 "Never say never, Little Critter," said Mrs. Critter. "You're doing your best, and I'm very proud of you. You just have to be patient. Blue will learn. I'm sure everything will be okay." Then she gave Little Critter a big hug.

7 "Thanks, Mom," said Little Critter. "You always make me feel better."

40

Knowing the Words

Write the story words that have these meanings.

1. complained

_____
(Par. 1)

2. not on top of

_____
(Par. 3)

Put a check by the meaning that fits the underlined word in each sentence.

3. Blue will never act <u>right</u>.

_____ correctly

_____ not left

4. Will Dad <u>play</u> with Blue?

_____ have fun

_____ a show

Reading and Thinking

1. How did Little Critter feel?

_____

_____

2. Who helped Little Critter feel better?

_____

_____

Write **R** by the sentences that are about **real** things. Write **M** by the sentences that are about **make-believe** things.

3. _____ People can make beds.

4. _____ Dogs can make beds.

5. _____ A cat wears pajamas.

6. _____ A person wears pajamas.

41

Blue Joins the Picnic

Read to see what Blue wants to eat.

1   The next evening, the Critter family had a picnic. They invited Gabby's family and Tiger's family. Maurice and Molly's family came, too. Mrs. Critter made potato salad and coleslaw. Gabby's dad made brownies. Tiger's mom and dad brought over a volleyball set. Maurice and Molly's parents made two kinds of cupcakes. Mr. Critter cooked hot dogs and hamburgers on the grill.

2   Little Critter and his friends played volleyball until it was time to eat. Blue played, too. He hit the ball with his head. He even got the ball over the net once. All the kids laughed.

3   "Who's ready for a hot dog?" asked Mr. Critter. "Come and get it!"

4   "I am," said Tiger. Mr. Critter picked up a hot dog with a fork. Before the hot dog made it to Tiger's plate, Blue jumped up and grabbed it in his mouth. Everyone laughed.

5   "No, Blue!" cried Little Critter.

6   "Sorry, Tiger," said Mr. Critter. "I'll get you another one."

7   "You did say come and get it," said Little Sister to Mr. Critter. "I guess Blue thought you meant him, too."

8   "I better take him to his doghouse for a while," said Little Critter. "We don't want to run out of hot dogs."

Reading and Thinking

Put each word in the right blank.

cooked   family   ready

1. Dad _____ on the grill.

2. Who is _____ for a hot dog?

3. Gabby's _____ came to the picnic.

Write **R** by the sentences that are about **real** things. Write **M** by the sentences about **make-believe** things.

4. _____ A hot dog can walk.

5. _____ A dog can walk.

6. _____ Birds can fly.

7. _____ Dogs can fly.

Working with Words

Circle the best word for each sentence. Then write it in the blank.

1. She likes to _____ flowers.

    pet   pan   pick

2. Sit _____ and read.

    back   bake   best

3. I like _____ book.

    think   thank   that

Fill in the missing vowel (**i**, **o**, or **u**) so the sentence makes sense.

4. Write on the l___ne.

5. Please give Blue a b_____ne.

6. May Blue _____se this bowl?

Fill in each blank with **str** or **spr** so the sentence makes sense.

7. Here is a ball of _____ing.

8. I will _____ay water on the grass.

9. Don't walk in the _____eet.

Shake, Blue

Read to see how Mr. Critter helps train Blue.

1   The next day, Little Critter and his friends met in the backyard for Blue's lesson. "Today we're going to teach Blue how to shake hands," said Gabby. She pointed to her dog training book. It showed a dog holding out his paw to a boy who was shaking it.

2   "How are you going to make Blue do that?" asked Little Sister.

3   "First, we have to show him how," said Gabby. She shook Little Sister's hand. Then Tiger and Little Critter shook hands. Maurice and Molly shook hands. Blue wagged his tail and barked.

4   Gabby took Blue's paw and said, "Shake, Blue." She did this three times. Then she told Little Critter to try. "Let Blue give you his paw by himself," she said.

5   Little Critter said, "Shake, Blue." Blue laid down on the ground. "Come on, Blue," said Little Critter. "Sit." Blue sat up. Before Little Critter could ask for his paw, Blue jumped on him.

6   Just then Mr. Critter came outside. He was holding something in his hand. "I think this might help," he said, handing the package to Little Critter. "Reward Blue with a hot dog when he does something right."

7   Gabby said, "Shake, Blue." Then she took his paw. Little Critter quickly gave Blue a piece of hot dog. Blue gobbled it down. After that, Little Critter asked Blue to shake. Blue stuck out his paw.

8   "Good dog!" cried Little Critter and all his friends. Little Critter gave Blue another piece of hot dog.

9   "That dog will do anything for a hot dog!" said Little Sister.

Reading and Thinking

Put each word in the right blank.

shake   piece   Reward

1. _____ Blue with a hot dog.

2. Blue ate a _____ of the hot dog.

3. Did Blue learn to _____ ?

Fill in the blanks.

4. Blue held out his paw, and Little Critter shook it.

   It stands for _____.

5. Gabby and Mr. Critter were happy because they were helping.

   They stands for _____ and _____.

6. Blue was carrying a bone as he ran.

   He stands for _____.

Working with Words

Circle the best word for each sentence. Then write it in the blank.

1. Did Gabby _____ Blue?

   day   tail   train

2. Can you _____ Blue bark?

   heel   hear   head

3. Put on your warm _____.

   coat   cook   clean

Change each underlined word to two words. Write them on the line.

4. Blue <u>didn't</u> want to learn.

   _____

5. This <u>isn't</u> my dog.

   _____

Circle the right letters to complete each word. Then write them in the blank.

6. Blue b___ked and wagged his tail.

   er   ar   ir

7. Training Blue is hard w___k.

   or   er   at

8. Gabby is a kind g___l.

   ir   er   ar

45

Lunch with Mrs. Crabtree

Read to see why the Critters invite Mrs. Crabtree for lunch.

1 "I have an idea," said Mrs. Critter one afternoon.

2 "What?" asked Little Critter and Little Sister.

3 "I think we should have Mrs. Crabtree over for lunch," said Mrs. Critter.

4 Little Critter and Little Sister both looked at their mom in surprise. "Mrs. Crabtree?" said Little Sister.

5 "Why?" asked Little Critter.

6 "Because she is our neighbor and our friend," answered Mrs. Critter.

7 "She won't be my friend," said Little Critter. "Because of Blue."

8 "That's not true," said Mrs. Critter. "Anyway, maybe Mrs. Crabtree will like Blue better if she gets to know him."

9 "Or maybe not," said Little Sister, giggling.

10 "I can make my famous peanut butter and pickle sandwiches," said Little Critter.

11 "Yuck!" said Little Sister. "Mrs. Crabtree would like jelly and potato chip sandwiches better."

12 "What about tuna fish?" said Mrs. Critter. "Everyone likes tuna fish!"

46

Knowing the Words

Write the story words that have these meanings.

1. meal at noon

_____
(Par. 3)

2. someone who lives nearby

_____
(Par. 6)

3. well-known

_____
(Par. 10)

Reading and Thinking

Put each word in the right blank.

idea   sandwiches   Everyone

1. We will have _____ for lunch.

2. Mrs. Critter told them her _____.

3. _____ likes tuna fish.

4. Write **1, 2,** and **3** by these sentences to show what happened first, next, and last.

_____ Little Critter asked "Why?".

_____ Little Sister wanted to make jelly and potato chip sandwiches.

_____ Mrs. Critter wanted to have Mrs. Crabtree over for lunch.

5. Why doesn't Little Critter think Mrs. Crabtree will be his friend?

_____

_____

6. What does Little Critter want to make for lunch?

_____

_____

47

Blue Makes Friends

Read to see how Blue tries to be friends with Mrs. Crabtree.

1. Mrs. Crabtree came for lunch the next day. Mrs. Critter made tuna fish sandwiches. She served them with potato chips and pickles. Mr. Critter made an apple pie for dessert. Everyone ate at the kitchen table. Blue sat quietly next to Mrs. Crabtree.

2. "Thank you so much for inviting me," said Mrs. Crabtree.

3. "I'm glad you could come," said Mrs. Critter.

4. "We're sorry about your roses," said Mr. Critter. "You know, Little Critter is working hard to train Blue. He's hoping to pay for your new roses very soon."

5. Just then Blue ran out of the kitchen. He came back with Little Sister's doll in his mouth. He dropped the doll next to Mrs. Crabtree.

6. "I see Blue knows how to carry things," said Mrs. Crabtree. Everyone laughed. Little Critter hoped Blue would keep behaving, but Blue ran out of the room again. This time, he came back with Little Critter's pajamas in his mouth. He dropped them next to Mrs. Crabtree. After that, he came back with a baseball glove, a teddy bear, and a towel. Blue sat down and looked up at Mrs. Crabtree.

7. "I think Blue is trying to be your friend, Mrs. Crabtree," said Little Critter.

8. "He can be my friend, as long as he doesn't dig up my new roses!" said Mrs. Crabtree.

Reading and Thinking

1. What did Blue bring to Mrs. Crabtree?

_____

_____

_____

2. Why did Blue bring things to Mrs. Crabtree? _____

_____

3. Do you think Mrs. Crabtree likes Blue now? _____

_____

Working with Words

Read each sentence and circle the word that is made of two shorter words. Write the two words on the lines.

1. Someone ate all the potato chips.

_____ _____

2. Blue made everyone laugh.

_____ _____

3. Where is the baseball glove?

_____ _____

Circle the best word for each sentence. Then write it in the blank.

4. Please _____ us a trick.

    who   show   those

5. Where are your _____ ?

    this   who's   shoes

6. Blue will _____ me.

    shook   chase   shout

Perfect Dogs

Read to see what Little Critter watches on TV.

1   Little Critter and Little Sister watched a dog show on TV. They saw beautiful dogs do many tricks. The owners walked their dogs around a ring. The judges made notes about each dog. None of the dogs were digging, howling, or snatching hot dogs. They sat when their owners said "sit." They walked nicely when their owners said "heel".

2   "Those dogs are perfect," said Little Sister. "Just like Fifi. I bet Su Su wins the $25 first prize."

3   "Blue," said Little Critter, "watch these dogs. Maybe you can learn something." Blue wasn't interested. He was busy chasing his tail.

4   Little Critter imagined the dog show. Blue listened. He sat. He heeled. He rolled over. He was perfect. He didn't even need hot dogs. Everyone clapped for Blue and Little Critter. The judges said Blue was the smartest dog they had ever seen. They put the first prize ribbon on Blue. Little Critter won the $25.

5   Little Critter's dream ended when he heard Blue barking. Little Critter and Little Sister ran to the window. Blue was sitting on the table and howling. Little Critter and Little Sister did not know why Blue was barking. There was nothing outside.

6   Little Sister laughed at Blue. She said, "Blue's sure not a show dog yet!"

Reading and Thinking

Look at each picture and circle the sentence that goes with it.

1. Blue likes to dig.

   Blue does not like to dig.

2. A mother can work.

   A mother can read.

3. He loves Blue.

   He doesn't like Blue.

4. What were Little Critter and Little Sister doing? _____

   _____

5. What did Little Critter imagine?

   _____

   _____

Working with Words

Write these sentences. Use one shorter word for the two words that are underlined.

1. She <u>does not</u> know my name.

   _____

   _____

2. Blue <u>will not</u> sit.

   _____

3. <u>It is</u> a beautiful day.

   _____

4. <u>I am</u> glad today.

   _____

Write these words so they mean more than one. One is done for you.

house _____ *houses* _____

5. ribbon _____

6. doll _____

7. window _____

Little Sister Speaks Up

Read to find out what Little Sister says to Su Su.

1 Day after day, Little Critter worked with Blue. Gabby always brought her dog training book. Maurice and Molly always brought hot dogs for Blue. Blue was learning little by little. Tiger cheered Blue on. Even Little Sister became hopeful for Blue.

2 One afternoon, Su Su walked by with Fifi. Fifi was wearing a fancy red polka-dot scarf.

3 "You're still trying to train that mutt?" asked Su Su. "He's too wild to be in a dog show."

4 Little Sister got mad. "Just because your dog is Miss Perfect doesn't mean you can make fun of Blue," she said.

5 Su Su just laughed. "We'll see who wins first prize," she said. Then she and Fifi walked away with their noses in the air.

6 "I want Blue to win just to make Su Su mad!" said Little Sister. Blue sat up and gave Little Sister his paw. "Maybe Blue *can* win the...." But Little Sister never finished her sentence. Blue jumped on her lap and licked her face. "Blue!" she cried. "Show dogs don't do this stuff!"

Knowing the Words

Write the story words that have these meanings.

1. wishing for _____
(Par. 1)

2. something worn on the neck

_____
(Par. 2)

3. ended _____
(Par. 6)

Put a check by the meaning that fits the underlined word in each sentence.

4. Blue <u>can</u> learn his lessons.

_____ a thing to hold food

_____ knows how to

5. I must <u>check</u> for the mail.

_____ make a line

_____ look with care

Reading and Thinking

1. Why was Little Sister mad?

_____

_____

2. Do you think Su Su's dog will win?

_____

Why or why not?

_____

3. Write **1**, **2**, and **3** by these sentences to show what happened first, next, and last.

_____ Little Sister got mad.

_____ Blue jumped on Little Sister.

_____ Su Su and Fifi walked by.

53

A Surprise for Blue

Read to see what Mr. and Mrs. Critter give Blue.

1   That night, Little Critter and Little Sister were sitting in the living room. They were taking turns brushing Blue. Blue was busy chewing a bone. Mr. and Mrs. Critter came into the room. Mrs. Critter was holding something behind her back.

2   "We have a surprise for Blue," said Mr. Critter. Mrs. Critter put a package in front of Blue. He sniffed it. Then he went back to his bone. Little Critter and Little Sister opened the package. Inside was a bright blue collar with Blue's name on it.

3   "Blue can wear this to the dog show," said Mr. Critter. "We're proud of you for working so hard with him. He's really learned a lot." Mrs. Critter said Blue would look very handsome in his new collar.

4   "Thanks," said Little Critter. "Blue sure has learned a lot."

5   Just then Blue stood up. He tried to dig a hole in the carpet. He wanted to bury his bone.

6   Little Sister said, "He hasn't learned to stop digging yet!"

54

Reading and Thinking

1. What was the surprise for Blue?

_____

_____

Put each word in the right blank.

surprise   collar   wear

2. Mr. and Mrs. Critter had a

_____ for Blue.

3. Blue got a new blue _____.

4. Blue will _____ his new collar.

Working with Words

The missing word in each sentence sounds like **stop**. Change the **st** in **stop** to **t**, **m**, or **p**. Write the new words and put them in the right sentences.

1. _____ _____ _____

2. Some popcorn didn't _____.

3. I hit the _____ of my head.

4. Clean the floor with a _____.

Circle the right letters for each sentence. Then write them in the blank.

5. They walked in the p_____k.

er   ir   ar

6. What happened f_____st?

ar   or   ir

Add **'s** to these words to show what belongs to each one.

7. dog   the _____ collar

8. cat   the _____ head

9. bird   the _____ nest

10. kitten the _____ ball

55

A Haircut for Blue

Read to see where Blue goes.

1   The dog show was the next day. The Critter family wanted to take Blue to get his hair cut. They climbed into the car, but Blue would not get in. Blue did not want to go.

2   "Come on, Blue!" said Little Critter. He and Little Sister tried to put Blue in the car. Blue jumped out of their arms and ran into the garage.

3   Mr. Critter got some hot dogs. Blue followed the smell of the hot dogs. Soon he was on his way to get a haircut.

4   In the waiting room, Blue hid under the chairs.

5   "My dog is not happy about getting a haircut," Little Critter told the dog groomer.

6   "Don't worry," said the dog groomer. She took Blue's leash. "He'll be just fine." She held out a treat and Blue followed.

7   When Blue was finished, the dog groomer brought him out. Blue was shiny clean and his fur was cut short. He smelled like flowers.

8   "Blue, you look like a show dog!" exclaimed Little Critter.

Knowing the Words

Write the story words that have these meanings.

1. place to keep a car _____
   (Par. 2)

2. went after _____
   (Par. 3)

Circle the three words in each line that belong together.

3. paws   tail   soft   head

4. glad   happy   pleased   sad

5. paint   grass   park   yard

Reading and Thinking

1. This story is mostly about

   _____ Blue's visit to the vet.
   _____ Blue's visit to the dog groomer.
   _____ Blue's visit to the pet store.

2. Why did the Critter family take Blue to be groomed? _____

   _____
   _____

3. What did Blue look like afterward?

   _____
   _____

4. Write **1**, **2**, and **3** to show what happened first, next, and last.

   _____ The dog groomer said, "He'll be just fine."
   _____ Blue was shiny clean.
   _____ Blue would not get in the car.

57

Another Bath

Read to see why Blue needs another bath.

1 Blue did not stay clean for long. When the Critter family got home, he raced out of the car. He headed right for the garden. Blue dug and dug. Dirt flew everywhere.

2 "It looks like Blue needs another bath," said Mr. Critter.

3 Little Critter looked at his dog and sighed. "I love you, Blue, but I wish you could stay clean for a little while."

4 "Don't worry, Little Critter," said Little Sister. "I'll help you give him another bath."

5 First, Little Critter and Little Sister hosed Blue off in the yard. Then they carried him upstairs to the bathroom. They shut the door so Blue couldn't run away. Little Critter filled the tub with warm water. Little Sister added some doggie shampoo. Blue wasn't happy.

6 "Let's scrub!" said Little Sister. They scrubbed the mud off Blue's face. They washed his paws. Blue splashed. He tried to jump out of the tub. Little Critter held Blue while Little Sister washed him.

7 When Blue was clean, they dried him off. Then, they put a T-shirt on him to keep his fur clean.

8 "Blue, you're not leaving the house until the dog show," said Little Critter. "No more digging today!"

1. What did Blue do when he got out of the car?

_____

2. What did Little Critter say to Blue?

_____

_____

Put each word in the right blank.

splashed   carried   shampoo

3. Little Critter and Little Sister
_____ Blue upstairs.

4. They washed Blue with _____.

5. Blue _____ in the tub.

Fill in the missing vowel (**a**, **i**, or **o**) so each sentence makes sense.

1. You did a f___ne job.

2. Wash off with the h___se.

3. We will m___ke the bed.

Use the underlined words to make a new word to finish each sentence.

4. A <u>tub</u> that you take a <u>bath</u> in is called a _____.

5. A <u>yard</u> that is in <u>back</u> of a house is called a _____.

Circle the best word for each sentence. Then write it in the blank.

6. Do not _____ at me.
show   shout   chair

7. Our dog is _____.
boat   clean   stay

The Dog Show

Read to see what the show dogs do.

1   The next morning, Little Critter put the new collar on Blue. He took off the T-shirt. Then he said, "Blue, I know you can be the winner." The Critter family got Blue into the car with no problems. They drove to the park.

2   Many people were already at the park to watch the dog show. Little Critter's friends were there to cheer for Blue.

3   "Good luck, Blue!" said Gabby and Tiger.

4   Maurice and Molly said, "We brought some hot dogs, just in case."

5   Little Critter watched the other dogs. He began to get nervous. Blue was number eight. After a while, Su Su and Fifi took their turn. Fifi wore a pink sweater with matching bows. She did all her tricks with no mistakes. Su Su smiled proudly when Fifi was finished.

6   The next dog took his turn. He was a beagle named Scout. Scout's owner had Scout sit, heel, speak, and roll over. Scout stood up on two legs and danced. Then he did a back flip. Finally, Scout carried a flower to the judges. Everyone clapped for Scout, even Su Su. It was Blue's turn next. Little Critter headed to the ring.

7   Mr. and Mrs. Critter wished Little Critter good luck.

8   Tiger and Little Sister shouted, "Go, Blue! Blue is number one!"

Reading and Thinking

Put each word in the right blank.

collar   clapped   brought

1. Little Critter put a new _____ on Blue.

2. Maurice and Molly _____ hot dogs.

3. Everyone _____ for Scout.

4. This story is mostly about

_____ what the dogs do at the dog show.

_____ what Tiger does at the dog show.

_____ what Little Sister does at the dog show.

Working with Words

To make a word mean more than one, add -es if the word ends in s, ss, ch, sh, or x. Write these words so that they mean more than one.

1. lunch _____

2. dish _____

3. box _____

Fill in the missing letter so the sentence makes sense.

4. I like to h____lp my dad.

5. Blue j____mped on Little Critter.

6. Little Critter p____cked up the ball.

Fill in the missing letters so each sentence makes sense.

ar   or   ur

7. Soon it will be Blue's t____n.

8. Can we play in the p____k?

61

Blue's Turn

Read to see what happens when Little Critter shows Blue.

1 Little Critter walked Blue around the ring. Little Critter was nervous. He had a funny feeling in his stomach. The judges told them to begin. Little Critter hoped Blue would listen.

2 "Sit, Blue," said Little Critter. Blue sat. "Good dog!" said Little Critter. "Shake, Blue." Blue gave his paw to Little Critter. "Good dog!" said Little Critter again.

3 Suddenly, Blue began to sniff. He tugged on the leash and pulled Little Critter around the ring. He sniffed and sniffed, his nose to the ground. "Stop, Blue!" cried Little Critter, but Blue would not listen. He started to dig a hole. Everyone at the show laughed. Little Critter knew he wouldn't win first prize.

4 "No, Blue!" yelled Little Critter just as Blue dug something up. It was an old metal box. The judges ran over to see.

5 One of the judges opened the box. Inside were many large, gold coins. "This dog has found a treasure," exclaimed the judge. "These are stolen coins. I believe they were taken from the Critterville Bank many years ago. Everyone thought the coins were gone for good. This dog is a hero!"

6 "Hooray for Blue!" cried Little Critter and all his friends.

Knowing the Words

Write the story words that have these meanings.

1. area for a show

_____
<small>(Par. 1)</small>

2. rope to hold an animal

_____
<small>(Par. 3)</small>

3. without warning

_____
<small>(Par. 3)</small>

4. tugged

_____
<small>(Par. 3)</small>

5. to smell

_____
<small>(Par. 3)</small>

Circle the three words in each line that belong together.

6. sit   heel   happy   shake

7. chair   table   mail   rug

8. box   brush   broom   mop

9. ran   sat   raced   chased

Reading and Thinking

1. Who opened the box?

_____

_____

2. Why was Blue a hero?

_____

_____

Look at each picture and circle the sentence that goes with it.

3. Blue is digging a hole.

Blue is opening the box.

4. Little Critter is happy.

Little Critter is angry.

Blue the Hero

Read to see how Blue becomes famous.

1   Scout won first prize, Fifi won second, but Blue was a hero. The gold coins Blue had found were stolen in the Great Critterville Bank Robbery. The bank gave Little Critter a $25 reward. People from the newspaper came to take pictures of Blue and Little Critter and their friends.

2   The reporter asked lots of questions about Blue. Little Critter told her they had been training him for weeks. "I was in charge of the lessons," Gabby said, "because I have this great dog training book." She held it up for the reporter to see. "We could never stop him from digging, though," added Tiger. "He loves to dig," said Molly. "Almost as much as he loves hot dogs," put in Maurice.

3   "This dog has an excellent sense of smell," said the reporter. "This time his digging made him a hero. We'd like to put a story about him on the front page."

4   Little Critter and his friends all smiled for the camera. Little Sister was very proud. "I always knew that dog would be famous!" she said.

64

Reading and Thinking

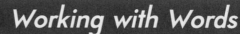

1. What was special about the coins Blue found?

_____

_____

2. What did the bank do?

_____

_____

3. Write **1**, **2**, and **3** to show what happened first, next, and last.

_____ Blue was a hero.

_____ Little Sister said she knew Blue would be famous.

_____ People from the newspaper came to see Little Critter.

Working with Words

In each row, circle the two letters in each word that make the same sound you hear in the underlined word.

toy   point   boy   noise

1. <u>show</u>   know   own   throw

2. <u>see</u>   tree   weeks   please

3. <u>found</u>   down   around   proud

4. <u>mean</u>   need   near   read

Circle the best word for each sentence. Then write it in the blank.

5. Do you like to play this _____?

same   game   name

6. Little Critter found _____ sister.

hit   him   his

7. This is my _____ trick.

best   nest   last

8. Little Sister hit the _____.

ball   call   tell

Circle each **c** that stands for the sound of **s** in these words.

9. once   12. piece

10. doctor   13. because

11. fence   14. come

A Party for Blue

Read to see who comes to celebrate with Blue.

1   The Critter family had a party for Blue. There was cake, ice cream, and, of course, hot dogs. The whole neighborhood was invited, including Su Su, Fifi, and Mrs. Crabtree.

2   "I'm sorry that Fifi didn't win first prize," said Little Critter.

3   "Next year, we will," said Su Su. "I'm teaching Fifi how to search for buried treasure." All the friends laughed.

4   "Blue is a hero," said Mrs. Crabtree to Little Critter. "Please bring him and your friends to my house tomorrow. I want to talk to you." Little Critter wondered what Mrs. Crabtree wanted. He was glad he had the reward money to pay for the roses.

5   When the party was almost over, a long, shiny black car drove up. The Mayor of Critterville stepped out. He said, "I am looking for a dog named Blue." Little Critter was so surprised he just stood there. Then he brought Blue over to the mayor. "I have a special medal for the hero of Critterville. Thank you, Blue, for finding the lost gold coins from the Critterville Bank Robbery." The mayor hung a medal around Blue's neck.

6   Everyone cheered. "Woof! Woof!" barked Blue.

Knowing the Words

Write the story words that have these meanings.

1. celebration

   _____
   (Par. 1)

2. look for

   _____
   (Par. 3)

3. the next day

   _____
   (Par. 4)

Circle the three words in each line that belong together.

4. heel   sit   stay   found

5. collar   leash   tag   bird

6. hat   walk   run   stay

7. mail   cake   ice cream hot dogs

Reading and Thinking

Look at each picture and circle the sentence that goes with it.

1. Blue and Fifi do not like each other.

   Blue and Fifi are friends.

2. Tiger likes hot dogs.

   Tiger does not like hot dogs.

3. Why do you think Mrs. Crabtree wants to speak with the friends?

   _____

4. Who gave Blue a medal?

   _____

   _____

Mrs. Crabtree's Idea

Read to see what Mrs. Crabtree tells the friends.

1   The next afternoon, Little Critter, Little Sister, Blue, and their friends went to see Mrs. Crabtree. They found her in her garden.

2   "Here's the money for your new roses," said Little Critter, holding out the reward money.

3   Mrs. Crabtree shook her head. "You keep it, Little Critter," she said. "I know how hard you and your friends worked to earn money for my new roses. I know about your lemonade stand. I know that is why you entered the dog show. There is another way you can repay me, though."

4   "How?" asked Little Critter.

5   "By helping me plant my new roses!" answered Mrs. Crabtree with a smile.

6   Little Critter was happy. "Guess who can dig the holes?" he said.

7   "Blue!" yelled all his friends.

8   Little Critter and his friends helped Mrs. Crabtree all afternoon. Blue dug the holes, and Little Critter and Gabby planted the roses. Maurice and Molly pulled weeds. Tiger

painted Mrs. Crabtree's fence. Little Sister swept the sidewalk and porch. When they were finished, Mrs. Crabtree made lemonade for everyone.

68

Reading and Thinking

1. This story is mostly about
   _____ how Mrs. Crabtree solves the problem.

   _____ how the friends make more money.

   _____ how Mrs. Critter solves the problem.

2. How did Little Critter pay Mrs. Crabtree back?

   _____

   _____

3. List three things the friends did for Mrs. Crabtree.

   _____
   _____

   _____
   _____

Working with Words

Circle the right letters for each sentence. Then write them in the blank.

1. Do you w____k hard?

   ar   or   ir

2. It is your t____n to play.

   ar   or   ur

3. They will help plant the g____den.

   er   or   ar

Circle the best word for each sentence. Then write it in the blank.

4. Can you make your _____?

   bag   bed   big

5. Gabby wrote a _____.

   listen   last   letter

6. We filled the _____ with milk.

   pan   pet   pop

Use the underlined words to make a new word to finish each sentence.

7. A <u>house</u> for a <u>dog</u> is called a

   _____.

8. A <u>walk</u> on the <u>side</u> of the street is called a _____.

Sweet Dreams for Little Critter and Blue

Read to see why everyone is happy.

1 Mrs. Crabtree thanked Little Critter and his friends for all their hard work. She was very happy about her rose garden. Her whole yard looked beautiful. "Thank you, too, Blue," she said and petted him. "You're a good dog."

2 "Good-bye, Mrs. Crabtree!" said all the friends.

3 Little Critter and Little Sister headed home. "I'm glad Mrs. Crabtree is our friend," said Little Critter. "I think she even likes Blue now."

4 "I think you're right," said Little Sister.

5 "Woof! Woof!" barked Blue.

6 After dinner, Little Critter went out to the doghouse. He brought Blue some dog food and some fresh water. They sat inside the doghouse together. "You know what, Blue?" said Little Critter. "You're the best dog in the whole wide world!" Little Critter yawned and put his arm around Blue.

7 Soon, Little Critter and Blue were fast asleep. Little Critter dreamed of gold coins and roses. Blue dreamed of hot dogs and digging.

Reading and Thinking

1. What did Little Critter say to Blue?

   _____

   _____

Fill in the blanks.

2. Tiger and Gabby talked as they worked.
   They stands for _____

   _____

3. Mrs. Crabtree answered, and she said, "Yes, Little Critter."
   She stands for _____

   _____

Working with Words

The missing word in each sentence sounds like **new**. Change the **n** in **new** to **bl, fl**, and **thr**. Write the new words, and put them in the right sentences.

1. _____ _____ _____

2. The wind _____ hard.

3. I _____ my dog a ball.

4. The bird _____ away.

Circle the best word for each sentence. Then write it in the blank.

5. Little Critter will _____ Blue.
   grass   brush   growl

6. Will Maurice and Molly _____ with us?
   dry   play   fry

The ending **-er** means "more" and the ending **-est** means "most." Add the endings **-er** and **-est** to these base words.

	-er	-est
clean	*cleaner*	*cleanest*
7. kind	_____	_____
8. fast	_____	_____

Packing Up

Read to find out what Little Critter packs for his visit.

1   One evening, the Critter family was eating dinner. Little Critter was playing with his mashed potatoes. Little Sister was rolling peas on her plate.

2   "Children, eat your food properly, please. Remember your good manners," said Mrs. Critter. Just then the telephone rang. Mr. Critter answered. "Hello, Grandpa, Mr. Critter said. "That sounds like a wonderful idea. Yes, we can drive out tomorrow morning."

3   Mr. Critter said, "Little Critter, Grandma and Grandpa would like to have you visit the farm for a week. Would you like that?"

4   Little Critter jumped out of his seat. "Yes! I'll go pack right now!"

5   Little Critter ran upstairs and found a bag to pack. He packed his racing car, his cowboy boots, his Super Critter costume, his toy trains, and his teddy bear.

6   He called downstairs. "Mom, will my bicycle and skateboard and football helmet fit in the car?"

7   Mrs. Critter came in Little Critter's room. "Little Critter, did you pack your toothbrush, socks, underwear, and pajamas?"

8   "Oops, guess I forgot about those things." said Little Critter.

Knowing the Words

Write the words from the story that have these meanings.

1. at night _____
(Par. 1)

2. put things in a bag _____
(Par. 4)

3. didn't remember _____
(Par. 8)

Working with Words

Circle the right word to finish the sentence. Then write the word in the blank.

1. The team ran a good _____.
   (face, case, race)

2. Hit the ball with the _____.
   (bell, bat, bed)

Reading and Thinking

1. Check the answer that tells what the story is mostly about.

   _____ good manners
   _____ packing for a trip
   _____ riding a bicycle

2. Look at the picture. Check the two sentences that tell about the picture.

   _____ Little Critter is packing.
   _____ Little Critter has cowboy boots.
   _____ Little Critter rides a bicycle.

3. Little Critter found a _____ to pack.

Some things are real and some are make-believe. Write **R** by real things. Write **M** by make-believe things.

4. _____ Teddy bears can talk.
5. _____ Children can learn.
6. _____ Skateboards can write.

What Will Little Critter Do at the Farm?

Read to see what Little Critter wants to do at the farm.

1   Mrs. Critter helped Little Critter pack his bag. She said, "Choose two of your favorite things to bring." Little Critter picked his cowboy boots and his teddy bear.

2   "Little Critter, we can put your bicycle on the back of the car, but you won't need your football helmet and skateboard at the farm."

3   "Okay, Mom. Grandpa and I will have lots to do anyway. We can go fishing, play baseball, ride the horses, and play checkers."

4   "Little Critter, you will have fun, but don't forget that a farm is a busy place. Grandma and Grandpa have a lot to do every day. Maybe you could help," said Mrs. Critter.

5   "Yes, I can help!" said Little Critter.

6   Little Sister popped into the room. "I can help, too! I want to go to the farm, too!"

7   Mrs. Critter said, "Little Sister, this time it's Little Critter's turn to visit. Next time it will be your turn. You will do fun things here at home."

8   "But I want my turn now!" said Little Sister.

9   Mr. Critter called upstairs, "Okay, everyone to bed early tonight. We have a long drive tomorrow!"

Knowing the Words

Write the words from the story that have these meanings.

1. thing you like best _____
   (Par. 1)

2. to take _____
   (Par. 1)

3. must have _____
   (Par. 2)

The words **come** and **go** have meanings so different that they are **opposite**. Make a line from each word in the first list to the word in the second list with the opposite meaning.

4. early   front
5. long   short
6. back   late

Working with Words

A word without any ending is a **base word**. The base word of **talking** is **talk**. Circle each base word below.

1. picks   2. helped   3. playing

Sometimes one word stands for two words. The word **didn't** stands for **did not**. Write a word from the story that can stand for each pair of words.

4. do not   _____
   (Par. 4)

5. it is   _____
   (Par. 7)

Reading and Thinking

1. Check the answer that tells what the story is mostly about.
   _____ Little Critter's teddy bear
   _____ what Little Critter will do at the farm
   _____ Little Sister's bicycle

2. What did Mrs. Critter help Little Critter do? _____
   _____

3. Check the sentence that tells what Little Sister wanted.
   _____ to play checkers
   _____ to go fishing
   _____ to go to the farm

4. Why did Mrs. Critter say Little Critter would not need his football helmet and skateboard?
   _____
   _____
   _____

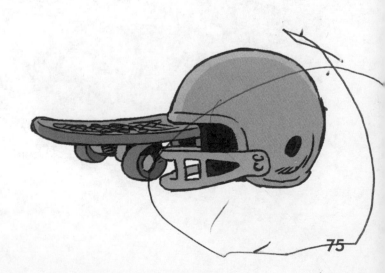

75

A Long Drive

Read to find out why it is a long trip.

1   The next morning, everyone got in the car and buckled their seat belts. Little Sister tried to bring her suitcase, but Mom said, "Next time, Little Sister."

2   After they were driving a short while, Little Sister said, "I have to go to the bathroom." Mr. Critter stopped at a McCritter's restaurant. Mrs. Critter took Little Sister inside.

3   The family drove on. Soon there were less buildings, fewer houses, and more green fields. "Farm country is beautiful, isn't it?" said Mrs. Critter.

4   Little Sister tapped Mom on the shoulder. "Mom, I have to go again."

5   "Okay, Honey, we'll stop as soon as we can."

6   This time, Mr. Critter stopped at a gas station. Mrs. Critter took Little Sister inside. "Dad, we're never going to get there!" said Little Critter.

7   "Sure, we will. We'll be there in no time," said Mr. Critter cheerfully. The Critters continued their trip. It was not long until Mrs. Critter felt another tap on her shoulder. It wasn't Little Sister this time.

8   "Okay, Little Critter, we'll stop as soon as we can," she said.

Knowing the Words

Write the words from the story that have these meanings.

1. one more time _____
(Par. 4)

2. in a happy way _____
(Par. 7)

3. top part of the arm _____
(Par. 7)

Circle the three words in each row that belong together.

4. morning   year   night   afternoon

5. coats   hats   feet   shoes

6. wet   cold   warm   hot

7. happy   sad   angry   old

Learning to Study

Number the words to show A-B-C order for each list.

1. _____ morning   2. _____ farm

_____ stop   _____ soon

_____ gas   _____ took

_____ can   _____ houses

Reading and Thinking

1. Check the answer that tells what the story is mostly about.

_____ a long drive

_____ Little Sister's suitcase

_____ Mr. Critter's seat belt

2. Why did Mr. Critter have to keep stopping?

_____

_____

_____

3. Little Critter thought they would never get to the _____.

Words such as **he**, **his**, **she**, and **her** take the place of other words. Read these sentences. Fill in the blanks.

4. Mr. Critter talked as he drove.
He stands for _____.

5. Little Critter packed his bag.
His stands for _____.

Write **R** by the real things. Write **M** by the make-believe things.

6. _____ Dogs ride bicycles.

7. _____ People drive cars.

Cleaning Up

Let's see how Little Critter helps out after lunch.

1 After a long drive, the Critters were very glad to be at the farm. Grandma and Grandpa were waiting on the front porch. They had a big lunch ready for the family. The Critters ate chicken soup and grilled cheese sandwiches, drank pink lemonade, and enjoyed chocolate cake for dessert.

2 "Grandma, I can help clean up!" said Little Critter. "I will wash the dishes."

3 "Why, that would be very nice of you, Little Critter," said Grandma.

4 Little Critter cleared the dirty dishes from the table. He only dropped one plate, one fork, and half a grilled cheese sandwich. He piled the dishes in the sink and ran warm water over them. Little Critter added some soap. Soon, there were soap bubbles flowing from the sink to the floor. Little Critter was very wet.

5 "I'm so glad I could help, Grandma!" said Little Critter, as he wiped some bubbles off his nose.

6 "I am too, Little Critter," replied Grandma. "But, we don't want you to do all the work by yourself!" Grandma and Mr. Critter decided they would help out, too.

Knowing the Words

Write the words from the story that have these meanings.

1. happy _____
   (Par. 1)

2. in between hot and cold _____
   (Par. 4)

Check the meaning that fits the underlined word in each sentence.

3. I won't <u>drop</u> the plate.
   _____ a little bit of water
   _____ to let go of

4. He put water in the <u>sink</u>.
   _____ part of the kitchen
   _____ to go under water

Working with Words

Write **S** beside each word that stands for one of something. Write **P** by each word that stands for more than one.

1. _____ dishes   2. _____ bubble

Circle the right word to finish each sentence. Then write the word in the blank.

3. Little Critter _____ how to help.
   (blew, knew, threw)

4. Don't _____ the water!
   (crash, flash, splash)

Reading and Thinking

1. What did Little Critter drop? _____

_____

_____

Write **T** if the sentence is true. Write **F** if it is not true.

2. _____ This story happens at the farm.

3. _____ Little Critter does not wash the dishes.

4. What did the Critters have for lunch? _____

_____

_____

_____

5. Why do you think Grandma and Mr. Critter helped out? _____

_____

_____

_____

6. How did Little Critter feel when he was helping? _____

_____

_____

Saying Good-bye

How does Little Critter feel when Mom and Dad leave?

1 Soon it was time for Mr. and Mrs. Critter and Little Sister to go home. Little Critter hugged his parents and his sister good-bye. He said, "Are you sure you have to leave now? Maybe you should all stay for the week, too!"

2 Mr. Critter said, "Little Critter, this is your special visit. Just you and Grandma and Grandpa. You will have lots of fun."

3 "Maybe I should go with you. Who is going to help Little Sister with her coloring books?" asked Little Critter.

4 "We will help her, Little Critter," answered Mrs. Critter.

5 "Oh no! I think I forgot my pajamas," said Little Critter.

6 "Honey, I packed those for you," said Mrs. Critter. "You will be fine."

7 Just then Grandpa came out with his checkers set. Grandpa had made the set himself. He had painted the checkers to look like chocolate and vanilla cookies. "Little Critter, how about a game of checkers?" asked Grandpa.

8 "Oh, boy! Checkers! I love these checkers!" said Little Critter, as he ran into Grandpa. Checkers flew everywhere. "Bye, Mom! Bye, Dad! Bye, Little Sister!"

9 "Good-bye, Little Critter. We'll see you soon."

80

Knowing the Words

Write the words from the story that have these meanings.

1. put your arms around

   _____

   (Par. 1)

2. clothes to wear to bed

   _____

   (Par. 5)

Words that mean the same or nearly the same are called **synonyms**. Circle two synonyms in each row.

3. begin   stop   call   start
4. be   leave   walk   go
5. listen   catch   see   look
6. rush   car   hurry   dog

Learning to Study

Number the words to show A-B-C order for each list.

1. _____ ask   2. _____ set
   _____ you   _____ fun
   _____ sister   _____ hug
   _____ came   _____ mom

Reading and Thinking

1. Check the answer that tells what the story is mostly about.

   _____ playing checkers

   _____ making a game

   _____ saying goodbye

2. Number the sentences to show what happened first, second, third, and last.

   _____ Grandpa asked Little Critter to play checkers.

   _____ Little Critter hugged his parents.

   _____ Little Critter thought he forgot his pajamas.

   _____ Little Critter ran into Grandpa.

Write the best word to finish each sentence below.

3. We saw the game and wanted to

   _____.

   (read, feel, play)

4. Grandpa _____ the checkers.

   (painted, tasted, jumped)

81

Taking Care of the Goats

Read to find out what Little Critter feeds to the goats.

1   After they said good-bye, Grandpa and Little Critter got to work. "First, we'll take care of the goats," said Grandpa.

2   "Are we going to feed them tin cans?" asked Little Critter. "I read a story at school about a goat that ate garbage."

3   "Well, Little Critter, goats can't really eat metal. They might like to chew the paper off of a can, though. They'll try to eat just about anything," said Grandpa.

4   Just then, the mother goat tried to munch on Little Critter's pants.

5   "Hey!" cried Little Critter. He tugged his leg away from the goat. Then, a baby goat started eating Little Critter's shirt.

6   "Let's get these goats some food quick!" said Grandpa.

7   Grandpa showed Little Critter the feed for the goats. It was a mix of hay and corn and a few vegetables. The baby goats ate right out of Little Critter's hand. Then they chased each other and jumped around the pen.

8   "Baby goats are funny!" said Little Critter.

9   "Baby goats are called kids," said Grandpa, "and the mother goat is called a nanny."

Knowing the Words

Write the words from the story that have these meanings.

1. something to throw away _____
(Par. 2)

2. move teeth _____
(Par. 3)

Write **S** for each pair of words that have the same or nearly the same meanings (synonyms). Write **O** for each pair with opposite meanings.

3. little _____ small

4. easy _____ hard

5. wash _____ clean

Circle the three words in each row that belong together.

6. goat   cow   pig   kangaroo

7. arm   hat   leg   foot

8. cup   pants   shirt   coat

Reading and Thinking

1. Number the sentences to show what happened first, second, third, and last.

_____ The mother goat chewed Little Critter's pants.

_____ Grandpa said that goats can't eat metal.

_____ The baby goat chewed Little Critter's shirt.

_____ The goats ate out of Little Critter's hand.

2. What was the goat feed made of?

_____

_____

_____

3. A baby goat is called a _____ and a mother goat is called a

_____.

Write the best word to finish each sentence below.

4. The goat was _____ Little Critter's shirt.
(eating, chasing, walking)

5. Little Critter _____ past the goat's pen.
(walked, pulled, called)

Bedtime

Read to see what helps Little Critter fall asleep.

1 Later that evening, Grandma showed Little Critter his room. "I get to sleep in that big bed?" asked Little Critter.

2 "Yes, it's all yours," said Grandma.

3 Little Critter climbed into the bed. Grandma tucked him under the patchwork quilt. "This bed is much bigger than my bed at home," he said.

4 "Good-night, Little Critter," said Grandma.

5 "Good-night, Grandma," replied Little Critter.

6 Grandma turned off the light. The room was much darker than Little Critter's room at home. "Grandma, I can't sleep. It's too dark," said Little Critter.

7 Grandma said, "Well, I'll turn on this night light for you, dear." Little Critter closed his eyes.

8 "Grandma, I still can't sleep," said Little Critter.

9 Grandma came into the room and turned on the light. "I know what's missing," she said. Grandma gave Little Critter his teddy bear. Little Critter hugged his bear as Grandma left the room again.

10 "I STILL can't sleep," called Little Critter.

11 This time Grandpa answered, "I know what will help, Little Critter. Come into the hallway."

12 Grandpa handed the telephone to Little Critter. "Hello?" he said, smiling. "Good-night, Mom." Little Critter was soon fast asleep.

Knowing the Words

Write the words from the story that have these meanings.

1. place to sleep _____
(Par. 1)

2. answered _____
(Par. 5)

Check the meaning that fits the underlined word in each sentence.

3. Grandma turned off the <u>light</u>.
_____ not heavy
_____ brightens a room

4. <u>Hand</u> me my teddy bear.
_____ part of the body
_____ give to

Working with Words

Write a word from the story that stands for each pair of words.

1. can not _____
(Par. 6)

2. I will _____
(Par. 7)

Reading and Thinking

1. Check two sentences that tell how Grandma helped Little Critter.
_____ She turned on the night light.
_____ She gave him his bicycle.
_____ She gave him his teddy bear.

2. How did Little Critter feel when it was time for bed? _____
_____

3. What did Grandpa do to help Little Critter feel better? _____
_____

4. Who did Little Critter talk to on the phone? _____
_____

Write the best word to finish each sentence below.

5. Grandma turned on the _____.
(night, light, bright)

6. Little Critter could not _____.
(sleep, slow, slip)

7. Grandma _____
Little Critter his room.
(turned, called, showed)

Early Morning

Read to see when the farm day begins.

1 Little Critter woke up to the sound of dishes clinking in the kitchen. He went into the bathroom. He washed his face, combed his fur, and brushed both of his teeth. He put on some clean clothes. His Critter watch said 7:00. Time for breakfast!

2 "Little Critter, I'll be in town most of the day, so you'll have to take care of Grandpa," said Grandma.

3 "Okay, Grandma," said Little Critter.

4 "Help yourself to breakfast, and I'll see you later," she said.

5 Little Critter ate a bowl of cereal and drank some juice. *I know,* he thought, *I'll make Grandpa some breakfast and bring it upstairs to him!*

6 Little Critter found a tray. He put some cereal, some milk, and some juice on the tray for Grandpa. Little Critter wobbled upstairs with the tray. But when he got there, the bed was made with no Grandpa in it.

7 As Little Critter was coming back downstairs, Grandpa walked in the kitchen door.

8 "Grandpa, I made you some breakfast!" said Little Critter.

9 "Well thanks, Little Critter, but I had breakfast two hours ago. You see, farm work starts very early around here!"

Knowing the Words

Write the words from the story that have these meanings.

1. noise _____
   (Par. 1)

2. morning meal _____
   (Par. 1)

3. animal hair _____
   (Par. 1)

4. a lot _____
   (Par. 2)

5. white liquid _____
   (Par. 6)

Circle the three words in each row that belong together.

6. breakfast lunch   food   dinner
7. milk   juice   water   cereal
8. bathroom   kitchen car   bedroom
9. brother   sister   father dog

Working with Words

Walk and **talk** are **rhyming words.** In rhyming words, only the beginning sound is different. Change the **f** in fine to **l**, **m**, or **n** to make rhyming words. Write each new word.

1. _____

2. _____

3. _____

Reading and Thinking

Words such as *he*, *she*, and *it* take the place of other words. Read these sentences. Then fill in the blanks.

1. Little Critter sang as he worked.
   He stands for _____.
2. Little Critter made breakfast and brought it upstairs.
   It stands for _____.

Write the best word to finish each sentence below.

3. I _____ to be at school on time.
   (ran, thought, ate)

4. The children moved the _____ to the backyard.
   (street, toys, stairs)

5. The _____ showed we were late.
   (flag, chicken, clock)

6. Check the sentence that tells why Grandpa was not in bed.
   _____ He went to town.
   _____ He was up early.
   _____ He was cooking breakfast.

87

The Pigpen

Read to find out how Little Critter helps with the pigs.

1 "Okay, Little Critter, let's feed the pigs," said Grandpa. Little Critter followed his grandfather to the pigpen. The pigs were rolling around in the mud. Little Critter held his nose. He looked around the pen. He saw one enormous mother pig, and he counted twelve squealing piglets. "Wow, Grandpa, that's a lot of baby pigs," said Little Critter, as he petted the soft, velvety hair of a piglet.

2 "Pigs have more babies than any other animal on the farm," said Grandpa, "and they're very smart animals."

3 Little Critter and Grandpa filled the pig troughs with slop. Grandpa said slop was made of all the scraps from the kitchen, like potato peels and apple cores. The heavy buckets of slop were almost as big as Little Critter. Little Critter and Grandpa gave the pigs water to drink and sprayed the ground with more water. "Those pigs love to play in the mud as much as I do," said Little Critter.

4 "They sure do. It helps keep the bugs off. Pigs stay cool by laying in the mud and the puddles," said Grandpa, "but, I think I know a better way for us to get cool."

Knowing the Words

Check the meaning that fits the under-lined word in each sentence.

1. Let's <u>feed</u> the pigs.
   _____ give food to
   _____ food for animals

2. <u>Bugs</u> bother pigs.
   _____ bothers
   _____ insects

Draw lines to match the words with opposite meanings.

3. enormous   on

4. off   warm

5. cool   tiny

Working with Words

Write a word from the story that can stand for each pair of words.

1. let us _____
   (Par. 1)

2. that is _____
   (Par. 1)

3. they are _____
   (Par. 2)

Make each word mean more than one by adding -s. Write the word.

4. piglet _____

5. bucket _____

Reading and Thinking

Write **R** by the real things. Write **M** by the make-believe things.

1. _____ Bugs laugh at pigs.
2. _____ Pigs roll in the mud.
3. _____ Pigs have babies.

Write the best word to finish each sentence below.

4. Little Critter _____
   twelve piglets.
   (counted, wanted, followed)

5. I'll _____
   my face and brush my fur.
   (light, move, wash)

6. Gabby _____
   the man play the game.
   (watched, told, filled)

7. We planted _____
   in the garden.
   (scraps, puddles, flowers)

89

Cooling Off

Read to see how Grandpa and Little Critter cool off.

1 After feeding the pigs, the chickens, and the turkeys, Little Critter and Grandpa put on their swimsuits.

2 "A little dip in the water will cool us off," said Grandpa. They walked down the hill to the pond. They put their towels down on the grass. Butterflies floated around the pond, and crickets chirped. The sun sparkled on the water.

3 Little Critter stuck his toe in the pond. A frog leaped over his foot. Little Critter jumped back. He looked down and saw tiny fish swimming around.

4 "You go in first, Grandpa," said Little Critter.

5 "Oh, frogs and fish won't hurt you, Little Critter," said Grandpa. "Maybe one day this week we can come down here and do some fishing."

6 "That would be great! I love fishing!" said Little Critter.

7 Grandpa jumped in the water and swam around. Little Critter paddled around after him. The cool water felt wonderful on such a hot, sticky day. They swam for just a few minutes.

8 "Well, Little Critter, I'm afraid that's all the time we have. Let's dry off, eat some lunch, and get back to work."

Knowing the Words

Words that mean the same or nearly the same are called **synonyms**. Use lines to match synonyms.

1. little   quick
2. close   tiny
3. fast   near

Working with Words

A **compound word** is made by putting two words together. Write a compound word for the underlined words below. One is done for you.

A word meaning <u>some</u> kind of <u>thing</u> is _____*something*_____.

1. A <u>suit</u> to <u>swim</u> in is a

    _____.

2. A time <u>after</u> the <u>noon</u> time is

    _____.

Fill in each blank with the right pair of letters to make a word.

        ch   sh   th   wh

3. _____ey   6. _____irped
4. lun_____   7. fi_____
5. _____eel   8. su_____

Reading and Thinking

1. What was Little Critter afraid of?

  _____

Write **R** by the real things. Write **M** by the make-believe things.

2. _____ Frogs can fly.
3. _____ Crickets chirp.
4. _____ Fish wear swimsuits.
5. _____ Butterflies fly.

6. Check the answer that tells what time of year it is in the story.

    _____ fall

    _____ summer

    _____ winter

Sandwiches for Grandpa

Read to see what Little Critter makes for lunch.

1 "Grandpa, since you didn't get to eat the breakfast I made you, maybe I can make you some lunch," said Little Critter.

2 "That's a fine idea, Little Critter," said Grandpa.

3 Little Critter went into the kitchen. He thought he would make his favorite kind of sandwiches for Grandpa.

4 First, Little Critter looked for the things he would need. He got orange juice and pickles out of the refrigerator. He found bread in the breadbox. He found some peanut butter and potato chips in the cupboard.

5 *This will be a delicious lunch, and I'm helping like Mom said,* he thought. *I can do this all by myself!*

6 Grandpa was waiting for him out on the front porch. Little Critter came out with two sandwiches and two glasses of milk.

7 "What did you make for us, Little Critter?" asked Grandpa.

8 "I made my famous peanut butter and pickle sandwiches with orange juice and potato chips!" he said. "Yum!"

9 "Yum-yum," said Grandpa. Then he took a small bite. He chewed very slowly.

10 "It's fun to be here with you, Grandpa," said Little Critter.

11 "It's fun to be with you too, Little Critter," said Grandpa.

Knowing the Words

Write the words from the story that have these meanings.

1. afternoon meal

   _____
   (Par. 1)

2. keeps food cold

   _____
   (Par. 4)

3. well known

   _____
   (Par. 8)

Circle the three words in each row that belong together.

4. pickles   orange juice   plates   bread

5. front   candy   side   back

6. milk   plates   dishes   bowls

Working with Words

A **compound word** is made by putting two words together. Use these words to make two compound words.

   fast   box   bread   break

1. _____   2. _____

Reading and Thinking

1. Check the answer that tells what the story is mostly about.

   _____ how to make a sandwich

   _____ what Little Critter makes for breakfast

   _____ what Little Critter makes for lunch

2. Write two things that Little Critter used to make the sandwiches.

   _____

   _____

   _____

3. Write **T** if the sentence is true. Write **F** if it is not true.

   _____ The story takes place at night.

   _____ Little Critter made his favorite lunch.

   _____ Little Critter was sad.

Write the best word to finish each sentence below.

4. The house was _____ after the party ended.
   (quiet, scared, angry)

5. My sister and her _____ took a trip.
   (field, friends, fence)

Milking the Cows

Read to see what Little Critter learns about cows.

1 "Little Critter, it's time to milk the cows again," said Grandpa.

2 "Why do you have to milk them *again*?" asked Little Critter.

3 "When a cow has a calf she makes milk for the baby. She makes so much extra milk that we must milk her twice a day."

4 Grandpa sat down on a stool and began to milk a cow named Jody. "On big farms, they have milking machines to do the work," said Grandpa. "Since we only have three cows at our little farm, Grandma and I can milk them."

5 Little Critter watched the milk stream into the bucket. Jody was very calm. Little Critter petted her smooth, brown coat as Grandpa milked. Little Critter fed her bunches of hay. "Boy, does she eat a lot!" he said.

6 "That's because cows have four stomachs," said Grandpa.

7 "Four stomachs! No wonder she eats so much!" said Little Critter.

8 "She makes milk from eating hay, grass, and grain," said Grandpa. "Milk is used to make things like cheese, butter, and yogurt."

9 "And ice cream!" said Little Critter. "Thanks for the ice cream, Jody!"

Knowing the Words

Write the words from the story that have these meanings.

1. baby cow _____
   (Par. 3)

2. not rough _____
   (Par. 5)

3. why _____
   (Par. 6)

4. a lot _____
   (Par. 7)

In each row, circle the two words with opposite meanings.

5. down   off   around   up
6. tell   went   say   came
7. show   large   small   grass

Working with Words

Circle the right word to finish each sentence. Then write the word in the blank.

1. My mother opened a _____
   of soup for lunch.
   (can   cane)

2. Will you _____
   the gift for the party?
   (hid   hide)

3. Does your new hat _____?
   (fit   fight)

Reading and Thinking

1. Check the answer that tells what the story is mostly about.
   _____ milking the cows
   _____ ice cream
   _____ milking machines

Write **T** if the sentence is true. Write **F** if it is not true.

2. _____ Grandma and Grandpa could milk all their cows.

3. _____ Little Critter was afraid to feed Jody.

4. Check the sentence that tells how cows and people are like each other.
   _____ They both have four legs.
   _____ They both have four stomachs.
   _____ They both have babies.

Write **R** by the real things. Write **M** by the make-believe things.

5. _____ Some farms use milking machines.

6. _____ Cows have five stomachs.

7. _____ Cheese can be made from milk.

Picking Berries

Read to see if Little Critter likes blackberries.

1   The next morning Grandpa went to town to buy farm supplies. Grandma woke Little Critter up early to help feed all the animals.

2   "Little Critter," said Grandma, "we have something really fun to do next." Grandma took two plastic bowls out of the cupboard. She handed one to Little Critter.

3   "What are we going to do with these bowls?" asked Little Critter.

4   "We're going to fill them with berries," said Grandma.

5   "Berries! Yum!" said Little Critter.

6   Little Critter and Grandma walked out to the blackberry patch behind the barn. The branches were filled with large, dark, purple berries.

7   "Pick the really dark ones," said Grandma. "Those are the sweetest!"

8   "Okay," said Little Critter as he picked a berry and ate it. A wonderful sweet flavor filled his mouth. "Mmmmm, these are so good."

9   "We need to fill these bowls so we can make pies for the Critter Country Fair tomorrow. We are going to enter the pie contest," said Grandma.

10   "Oh, boy, a pie contest! I can't wait," said Little Critter.

11   Little Critter started picking berries, but he couldn't resist tasting them. After a while, Grandma's bowl was almost full. "How are you doing, Little Critter?" asked Grandma. She looked at his bowl. "I think there are more berries in your belly than in your bowl!"

Knowing the Words

Write the words from the story that have these meanings.

1. in back of

   _____
   (Par. 6)

2. what something tastes like

   _____
   (Par. 8)

Check the meaning that fits the underlined word in each sentence.

3. Little Critter went to the blackberry <u>patch</u>.

   _____ to fix a hole in something

   _____ a small area

4. Little Critter <u>picked</u> blackberries.

   _____ gather from trees

   _____ collected

Working with Words

Write a word from the story that can stand for each pair of words.

1. We are _____
   (Par. 4)

2. cannot _____
   (Par. 10)

An **'s** shows that a thing belongs to someone. Change these words to show what belongs to someone.

3. Grandma_____ bowl

4. Grandpa_____ berries

Reading and Thinking

1. Who picked more berries?

   _____

   _____

2. What kind of berries did Little Critter and Grandma pick?

   _____

3. Why wasn't Little Critter's bowl full?

   _____

Write **T** if the sentence is true. Write **F** if it is not true.

4. _____ Grandma wanted to make pies.

5. _____ Little Critter did not eat any berries.

6. _____ Little Critter does not like berries.

Baking Pies

Read about the two bakers.

1 Grandma and Little Critter washed the blackberries in the kitchen sink. They mixed the berries with sugar to fill the pie. Grandma got out the flour and shortening to make dough for the crust.

2 "Little Critter, we need to roll out this dough to make the crust," said Grandma. Grandma showed Little Critter how to roll out the dough smooth and flat. They put one half of the dough in the bottom of the pie plate. Then Grandma let Little Critter pour in the berries.

3 "Grandma, this is going to be the best pie at the Critter Country Fair!" said Little Critter.

4 "I don't know about that, Little Critter. There are going to be a lot of delicious pies in the contest," said Grandma.

5 They put the other piece of dough over the top of the berries. Grandma showed Little Critter how to squeeze the edges of the dough together so the berries wouldn't leak out. Little Critter made the extra dough into heart shapes to decorate the top.

6 After that, Grandma and Little Critter made two more pies.

7 "Good work, Little Critter! I will put the last pie in the oven," said Grandma.

Knowing the Words

Write the words from the story that have these meanings.

1. put two different things together

_____
(Par. 1)

2. tastes very good _____
(Par. 4)

3. Check the meaning that fits the underlined word in the sentence.

Little Critter put hearts on <u>top</u> of the pie.

_____ a toy that spins

_____ highest part

Learning to Study

To put words in A-B-C order you must first look at the first letter of each word. If the first letters are the same, look at the second letters. Number each list to show A-B-C order.

1. _____ flour   **2.** _____ pie

_____ berries   _____ plate

_____ crust   _____ pour

_____ oven   _____ put

Reading and Thinking

1. Check the answer that tells what the story is mostly about.

_____ baking blackberry pies

_____ turning on the oven

_____ washing blackberries

2. Number the sentences to show what happened first, second, third, and last.

_____ They put the last pie in the oven.

_____ Little Critter decorated the top of the pie.

_____ Grandma got the flour out of the cupboard.

_____ Grandma and Little Critter washed the berries.

Write **T** if the sentence is true. Write **F** if it is not true.

3. _____ Pie crust is made of flour and shortening.

_____ Pies do not need to be baked.

4. What did Grandma teach Little Critter about making a pie?

Picking Vegetables

Read to find out what the Critters will have for dinner.

1   When the pies were done, Grandma and Little Critter headed out to the vegetable garden with a big basket.

2   "Let's pick some potatoes for dinner tonight," said Grandma.

3   Little Critter looked around, "I don't see any potatoes."

4   "Potatoes are a root vegetable. They grow underground, just like carrots and beets," said Grandma. Together, Little Critter and Grandma dug up some potatoes and some carrots.

5   Grandma said, "The green tomatoes aren't quite ready to eat yet. Pick some nice, ripe, red ones. Did you know every flower on that tomato plant will become a tomato? It's like magic, isn't it, Little Critter?"

6   "A flower turning into a tomato *is* magic!" said Little Critter, as he pulled the bright tomatoes off the plants.

7   Little Critter and his grandma added lettuce, green beans, and purple beets to their basket. Little Critter thought, *I'll bet those purple beets taste sweet like the blackberries! Yum.*

8   "Grandma, don't you have any pumpkins growing? We can make pumpkin pies next!"

9   Grandma sighed. "Oh, my! Pumpkins won't be ready until fall, Little Critter," she said. "Besides, we've got an awful lot of blackberry pie to eat first!"

Knowing the Words

Write the words from the story that have these meanings.

1. place where things grow _____
(Par. 1)

2. ready to eat _____
(Par. 5)

Circle the three words in each row that belong together.

3. nap   dream   sight   sleep
4. beets   potatoes   carrots   flowers
5. sky   trees   flowers   plants

Working with Words

Write the best word to finish each sentence below.

1. Do you _____ the new teacher?
(know, nose, noise)

2. Did someone _____ on the door?
(nest, lock, knock)

Write these compound words beside their meanings.

underground   blackberry
afternoon

3. a berry that is black _____
4. later than noon _____
5. under the ground _____

Reading and Thinking

1. What color are tomatoes that are not ready to eat? _____ _____

2. Check two sentences that show that potatoes grow underground.
_____ Potatoes taste good.
_____ Little Critter did not see any potatoes above the ground.
_____ Little Critter dug up the potatoes.

3. How are carrots like potatoes?
_____

Write **R** by the real things. Write **M** by the make-believe things.

4. _____ Potatoes can walk.
_____ Vegetables grow in the garden.
_____ Little Critter is a pumpkin.

Veggies for Dinner

Read to find out if Little Critter likes a new vegetable.

1 "Please pass the potatoes," said Little Critter.

2 "Why, you have such nice manners, Little Critter," said Grandpa.

3 "We learned about good manners in school," said Little Critter. "Did you have a good day, Grandpa?"

4 "I had a very good day in town," said Grandpa. "I got some new tools, some feed, and I bought a few new hens."

5 "I helped Grandma today," said Little Critter.

6 "You sure did," answered Grandma. "I'm just surprised you don't have a tummy ache from eating all those blackberries."

7 "Please pass the beets," said Little Critter.

8 "Oh, these fresh beets are delicious!" said Grandma.

9 Little Critter was ready for a wonderful, sweet bite. But, when he tasted the beets, they were not sweet. They were sour. They did not taste good. Little Critter remembered his manners. He chewed very slowly and swallowed.

10 "I thought these would taste like berries," said Little Critter with a frown.

11 Grandma and Grandpa smiled at each other. "I didn't like beets either when I was your age," said Grandpa. "I have an after-dinner treat for you that might be better." Grandpa got up and handed Little Critter a purple stick of candy.

12 "Oh!" exclaimed Little Critter. "This will taste much better than beets!"

Knowing the Words

Write the words from the story that have these meanings.

1. being polite _____
   (Par. 2)

2. pain _____
   (Par. 6)

3. not sweet _____
   (Par. 9)

Circle the three words in each row that belong together.

4. taste   eat   chew   move

5. wonderful   sour   delicious   good

Working with Words

In each sentence, circle three words with the same vowel sound as the word in dark print.

1. **now**   The cow found the sweet grass and gave a loud MOO!

2. **now**   How can I drive around the mountain?

Reading and Thinking

1. Check the answer that tells what the story is mostly about.

   _____ Little Critter doesn't like vegetables.

   _____ Little Critter tries a new vegetable.

   _____ Grandpa bought new hens in town.

2. What did Little Critter think beets would taste like? Why?

   _____

   _____

   _____

   _____

3. How do you know that Grandma likes beets? _____

   _____

Write **T** if the sentence is true. Write **F** if it is not true.

4. _____ Little Critter likes beets.

   _____ Grandma likes beets.

   _____ Grandpa gave Little Critter some candy.

5. Check two answers that describe Little Critter.

   _____ He is mean.

   _____ He helps out.

   _____ He has good manners.

The Critter Country Fair

Read to see what is going on at the fair.

1 It was a hot, bright summer morning. Little Critter and his grandparents headed for the Critter Country Fair.

2 When they arrived, Little Critter looked all around. The rides whirled. The animals *mooed* and *crowed* and *baaed* in the barns. Music played loudly. Fair workers called out to come play their games. There were contests to show off garden vegetables, fresh-baked pies, and homemade jars of jelly. The warm air smelled of sweet cotton candy and spicy mustard.

3 Grandma needed to bring their pie to the cooking tent. The pie would be kept in a cool place until it was time for the contest.

4 "What should we do, Little Critter?" asked Grandpa, as he wiped his brow.

5 "Let's play a game, Grandpa!" said Little Critter. "Let's play that game where you spray water in the clown's mouth and blow up a balloon."

6 Little Critter and Grandpa sat down at the game. Little Critter held his sprayer tightly and aimed at the clown's mouth. He turned to talk to Grandpa when suddenly the game began! Little Critter sprayed water all over Grandpa's shirt instead of in the clown's mouth.

7 "Well, Little Critter, that's one way to cool off!" said Grandpa.

Knowing the Words

In each row, circle two words that have opposite meanings.

1. see   close   far   look
2. never   few   always some
3. cry   break   sleep   wake

Working with Words

A word part that can be said by itself is called a **syllable**. Some words have two consonants between two vowels. These words can be divided between the consonants, as in **pic|nic**. In each word below, draw a line to divide the word into syllables.

1. s u m m e r   3. c o t t o n
2. s u d d e n   4. c o n t e s t

Walk and **talk** are **rhyming words**. In rhyming words, only the beginning sound is different. Write words that rhyme with **spray** by changing **spr** in **spray** to **p** or **w**.

5. _____   6. _____

Then use each new word in the right sentence.

7. Grandpa will show you the _____ to the fair.
8. We must _____ for our tickets.

Reading and Thinking

1. Check the answer that tells what the story is mostly about.
   _____ the pie contest
   _____ cotton candy
   _____ the fair

Write the best word to finish each sentence below.

2. I want to play that _____ with Grandpa. (warm, game, tent)

3. Little Critter looked all _____ the fair. (around, above, behind)

4. The clown had a bright red
   _____.
   (jelly, garden, mouth)

Read these sentences. Then fill in the blanks.

5. Grandpa sneezed as he played the game.
   He stands for _____.

6. Grandma heard music as she walked by the tent.
   She stands for _____.

7. The ice cream melted as it sat on the table.
   It stands for _____.

The Twisty Teacup

Read to see if the Twisty Teacup is a fun ride.

1 "Grandpa, let's go on a ride now!" said Little Critter.

2 "Which ride would you like to go on?" asked Grandpa. "How about the merry-go-round?"

3 "The merry-go-round is for critters littler than me. I want to go on the Twisty Teacup ride!" said Little Critter.

4 "Okay, Little Critter. That ride spins an awful lot. I will stay here and watch you," said Grandpa.

5 Little Critter got in line with the other critters. He gave the fair worker his ticket. As Little Critter sat in a teacup, another fair worker fastened his safety belt . He held on tightly. The ride began slowly. *This is nothing*, Little Critter thought to himself. *I won't get dizzy.*

6 Just then the ride sped up. The teacup whirled Little Critter around in circles. The kids around him squealed. "Whoooaaaa!" screamed Little Critter. He closed his eyes, but that made him feel more dizzy.

7 Little Critter was very happy when the ride was over. Everything was still spinning when he stumbled out of the teacup.

8 "You look a little pale. Are you okay, Little Critter?" asked Grandpa.

9 Little Critter wobbled. "I think so Grandpa, but maybe we should go on the merry-go-round next time!" said Little Critter.

Knowing the Words

Words that mean the same or nearly the same are called **synonyms**. Circle two synonyms in each row.

1. scream   ride   spin   yell
2. worker   belt   strap   stay
3. glad   sad   wobble   happy

Working with Words

Words that end in **s**, **ss**, **x**, **sh**, or **ch** add **-es** to show more than one. Rewrite these words to show more than one. One is done for you.

dress   _dresses_

1. box   _____
2. kiss   _____
3. watch   _____

Circle the right word to finish each sentence. Then write the word in the blank.

4. He _____ his bicycle around the farm. (rod   rode)

5. Little Critter wanted some _____ in his soda pop. (is   ice)

6. That _____ makes me dizzy. (ride   rid)

Reading and Thinking

1. Number the sentences to show what happened first, second, third, and last.

_____ Grandpa asked Little Critter if he was okay.

_____ Little Critter did not want to ride the merry-go-round.

_____ The fair worker fastened Little Critter's safety belt.

_____ Little Critter was happy when the ride was over.

2. Why did Little Critter feel dizzy?

_____

_____

Write **T** if the sentence is true. Write **F** if it is not true.

3. _____ The ride was called the Tiny Teacup.

4. _____ Grandpa did not go on the ride.

5. _____ Little Critter was the only one on the ride.

6. Why didn't Little Critter want to go on the merry-go-round at first?

_____

_____

7. What changed his mind?

_____

_____

Two Pie Contests

Read to see why Little Critter isn't hungry for pie.

1   Little Critter, Grandma, and Grandpa entered the cooking tent just as the pie contest began. The judges were tasting each pie and making notes. Little Critter's stomach growled. He saw a sign in the next tent for a different kind of pie contest.

2   "Grandma, can I go watch the pie-eating contest?" asked Little Critter.

3   "Sure," said Grandma. "Then come back here afterwards."

4   When Little Critter walked into the tent, someone announced, "The pie-eating contest will now begin. All contestants to the front table, please."

5   The smell of pie made Little Critter's stomach growl even more. He sat down at the table. Someone placed a cherry pie in front of him.

6   "On your mark, get set, go!" Little Critter was busy looking for his fork while the other contestants stuck their faces in their pies! Little Critter did the same. He ate and ate, but he could not finish. The winner had eaten five pies!

7   Little Critter rubbed his tummy. He tried to wipe the sticky cherries off his fur and his clothes. He dragged himself back to the cooking tent. Grandma was holding a piece of the pie she and Little Critter had made. It had a red ribbon on it.

8   "We took second place, Little Critter!" said Grandma. "Look! I saved you a nice, big piece!"

Knowing the Words

Check the meaning that fits the underlined word in each sentence.

1. Can I go <u>watch</u> the pie-eating contest?
   _____ small clock
   _____ look at

2. I will <u>save</u> you a piece of pie.
   _____ set aside
   _____ rescue

3. Did she <u>run</u> in the race?
   _____ move fast on legs
   _____ what a machine does

Learning to Study

To put words in A-B-C order you must first look at the first letter of each word. If the first letters are the same, look at the second letters. Number each list to show A-B-C order.

1. _____ sign
   _____ stomach
   _____ saved
   _____ set

3. _____ tent
   _____ tasting
   _____ begin
   _____ their

2. _____ pie
   _____ faces
   _____ contest
   _____ judges

4. _____ red
   _____ fur
   _____ ribbon
   _____ read

Reading and Thinking

Use the groups of words in the box to finish the sentences below.

> • she thought he would like to eat it
> • he was hungry
> • he smelled pie

1. Little Critter ate the cherry pie because _____.

2. Little Critter's stomach growled louder when _____.

3. Grandma saved a piece of pie for Little Critter because ____
   _____
   _____.

A Letter from Mom and Dad

Read to see what Mr. and Mrs. Critter write.

1 When Grandma, Grandpa, and Little Critter got home from the country fair, they found a letter for Little Critter in the mailbox. Little Critter read it out loud to his grandparents.

2 Dear Little Critter,

We are glad that you are having fun at the farm. It sounds like you are learning a lot about farm life. Which animals are your favorites?

3 Yesterday, we took Little Sister to the zoo. She liked the elephants the best. After the zoo, we all got some ice cream. The weather has been very warm. No wonder you and Grandpa jumped in the pond!

4 You are a big help to your grandparents. Grandma and Grandpa are happy to have you there.

5 We miss you a lot. But, we'll see you in just a couple of days. You can tell us more about your visit!

> Love,
>
> Mom and Dad

6 P.S.: Little Sister misses you a lot, too!

7 Grandpa said, "We sure are glad to have you, Little Critter. We will miss you when you go home."

8 Little Critter said, "I like being here, too. Just me and my grandma and my grandpa."

Knowing the Words

Write the words from the story that have these meanings.

1. place to deliver letters _____ (Par. 1)

2. like the most _____ (Par. 2)

3. day before today _____ (Par. 3)

In each row, circle the two words with opposite meanings.

4. close   tiny   far   little

5. hot   cold   tiny   ice

6. smooth   hardest   softest   loudest

Working with Words

The ending -**er** means "more," so **prouder** means "more proud." The ending -**est** means "most," so **proudest** means "most proud." Add the endings -**er** and -**est** to these base words. One is done for you.

Malcolm is the tall*est* of six boys.

1. Little Critter is old____ than Little Sister.

2. I was the loud____ of the four.

Reading and Thinking

1. Write two things that Little Critter's mom and dad wrote about in their letter.

_____

_____

_____

_____

Write **T** if the sentence is true. Write **F** if it is not true.

2. _____ Little Critter is having fun at the farm.

3. _____ Little Sister is at the farm.

4. _____ Little Critter's family misses him.

5. _____ Little Critter does not help Grandma and Grandpa.

6. _____ Grandma and Grandpa are glad to have Little Critter visit.

7. Mom, Dad, and Little Sister went to the _____ and got some _____ afterwards.

Write the best word to finish each sentence.

8. Grandma _____ a letter in the mailbox. (found, hid, woke)

9. The girl _____ her hand to show she was ready. (washed, bit, waved)

Stormy Night

Read to find out how Grandpa helps Little Critter.

1 Little Critter was getting ready for bed when there was a loud crash of thunder. Little Critter dove under the bed and closed his eyes.

2 Grandpa came into the room. "Are you afraid of the storm?"

3 "I hate thunder and lightning," said Little Critter as he came out from under the bed.

4 "You are safe inside, Little Critter," said Grandpa. "We need rain so our crops will grow."

5 The thunder boomed again and the lightning flashed. Little Critter covered his face.

6 "Were you scared of storms when you were little, Grandpa?" asked Little Critter.

7 "Yes," said Grandpa.

8 "How come you aren't afraid now?" asked Little Critter.

9 "One time I watched a thunderstorm with my grandpa. At first, I closed my eyes. Then I found out that if I watched the lightning, I wasn't so scared," said Grandpa.

10 Little Critter and Grandpa listened to the rain hitting the window. The next time the lightning flashed, Little Critter tried not to close his eyes. He squeezed Grandpa's hand. The lightning lit up the farmyard.

11 In a little while, the thunder wasn't so loud anymore. The lightning wasn't so bright.

12 "Grandpa, I think I'm not scared anymore," said Little Critter.

13 "Good night, Little Critter," said Grandpa. "Call if you need me."

14 "Good night, Grandpa," said Little Critter.

Knowing the Words

Write the words from the story that have these meanings.

1. shut _____
   (Par. 1)

2. hard rain _____
   (Par. 2)

3. scared _____
   (Par. 8)

Check the meaning that fits the underlined word in each sentence.

4. You are <u>safe</u> inside.

   _____ place to keep money

   _____ won't be hurt

5. I'm glad the storm is <u>over</u>.

   _____ on the other side

   _____ done, finished

6. My <u>ears</u> hurt from the noise.

   _____ parts of corn plants

   _____ things used for hearing

Learning to Study

Number the words to show A-B-C order for each list.

1. _____ thunder   2. _____ need

   _____ here   _____ night

   _____ hard   _____ eyes

   _____ storm   _____ now

Reading and Thinking

1. Number the sentences to show what happened first, second, third, and last.

   _____ Little Critter dove under the bed.

   _____ There was a loud crash of thunder.

   _____ Little Critter wasn't scared anymore.

   _____ Grandpa told Little Critter a story.

2. Check two answers that show Little Critter was scared.

   _____ Little Critter squeezed Grandpa's hand.

   _____ Little Critter went to sleep.

   _____ Little Critter dove under the bed.

Write **R** by the real things. Write **M** by the make-believe things.

3. _____ Thunder is a loud noise.

4. _____ A storm can laugh.

Write the best word to finish each sentence below.

5. Thunder can be very _____.
   (loud, flat, bright)

6. Lightning can be very _____.
   (loud, bright, furry)

Riding the Horses

Read to see what Little Critter learns about horses.

1 The next day, Little Critter and Grandpa took care of the horses. They fed the horses hay, cleaned out their stalls, and brushed their coats.

2 Little Critter was brushing a horse called Buttercup. "You are such a nice horse," said Little Critter, as he petted her softly.

3 "Horses like it when you talk to them," said Grandpa. Grandpa was grooming a very big horse named Old Kicker.

4 Grandpa showed Little Critter how the horses wore horseshoes. "Does it hurt when they nail those horseshoes onto their hooves?" asked Little Critter.

5 "No, it doesn't hurt them at all. Horseshoes help protect the horses' hooves," said Grandpa. "Let's take these horses out for some exercise."

6 Grandpa strapped a leather saddle on each horse. Then he said, "Use the reins to guide your horse. Pull gently on the right rein to turn to the right. Pull on the left rein to steer left. Pull back on both reins and say 'Whoa' to stop the horse," said Grandpa. "I think we are about ready for our ride."

7 "I want to ride Old Kicker!" said Little Critter.

8 Old Kicker jumped on his hind legs and whinnied loudly.

9 "Maybe you should ride Buttercup today, Little Critter!" exclaimed Grandpa.

Knowing the Words

Write the words from the story that have these meanings.

1. keep safe _____
   (Par. 5)

2. seat put on a horse _____
   (Par. 6)

Working with Words

Write the best word to finish each sentence below.

1. Storms can bring _____ .
   (rain, ran, run)

2. Can you _____ the new word?
   (said, sad, say)

3. I _____ the answer.
   (now, know, not)

An **'s** at the end of a word shows that a thing belongs to someone or something. Change these groups of words by using **'s.**

4. the saddle of the horse

   the _____ saddle

5. the farm of Grandpa

   _____ farm

Reading and Thinking

1. What did Grandpa say did not hurt the horses?

   _____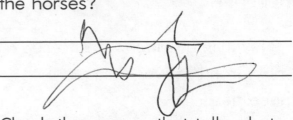
   _____

2. Check the answer that tells what the story is mostly about.
   _____ how to put shoes on horses
   _____ taking care of horses
   _____ Old Kicker

3. Check two sentences that tell why Little Critter may not want to ride Old Kicker.

   _✓_ Old Kicker whinnied loudly.

   _✗_ Old Kicker had a saddle on.

   _✓_ Old Kicker jumped up on his hind legs.

4. List two things that can be done to care for horses.

Shearing the Sheep

Read to see who Little Critter plays with.

1   Next, Little Critter went to see what Grandma was doing in the sheep pen.

2   "Why are you feeding that baby sheep with a bottle, Grandma?" asked Little Critter.

3   "Sometimes we have to help the ewes feed their babies," said Grandma.

4   "Ewes?" asked Little Critter.

5   "Mother sheep are called *ewes*," said Grandma. "Would you like to take care of this baby? I am going to shear its mother."

6   "Shear?" asked Little Critter.

7   "Yes, I am going to shave the wool off this sheep. Then we will sell the wool. Things like sweaters and blankets are made of wool," said Grandma. "Take this bottle of milk. You can finish feeding this lamb."

8   When Grandma took the ewe into the barn, the little lamb bleated loudly. Little Critter fed the lamb the bottle of milk. The hungry lamb drank it quickly. Little Critter walked around the pen. The lamb followed him, looking for more milk. Little Critter ran to the other side of the pen, and the playful lamb dashed after him. They chased each other back and forth.

9   When Grandma brought the ewe back to the pen, the little lamb ran straight to her mother.

10   "I guess our game of tag is over!" said Little Critter.

Reading and Thinking

1. Check the answer that tells what the story is mostly about.
   _____ making wool blankets
   _____ cleaning the sheep pen
   _____ learning about sheep

Read these sentences. Then fill in the blanks.

2. Grandma talked while she sheared the sheep.
   She stands for _____.

3. The lamb pulled the bottle as it drank.
   It stands for _____.

4. Little Critter laughed as he chased the lamb.
   He stands for _____.

Working with Words

Write the best word to finish each sentence below.

1. I have a _____ on my dress.
   (pen, pine, pin)
2. Can you _____ the horse?
   (ride, red, roll)
3. That book is _____.
   (win, mine, men)
4. Will you feed the _____?
   (can, car, cat)
5. The boys _____ their lunch.
   (cook, look, book)

When **re-** is added to a word, it changes the meaning of the word. The word part **re-** means "again." **Refill** means "fill again." Add **re-** to these words to finish the sentences.

6. I will _____build the house.

7. Who will _____do these papers?

8. Please _____fill the tall jar.

9. Did you _____write the test?

10. Did the station _____run the show?

11. Please _____tell the story.

117

A Bicycle Ride

Read to find out what Little Critter sees on his bicycle ride.

1 "Grandma, do you want to go on a bike ride?" asked Little Critter.

2 "Honey, I'd like to, but I've got some things to do here," said Grandma.

3 "Grandpa, how about you?" asked Little Critter.

4 "I've got some chores to finish up, Little Critter. You may go. Just stay on the paths here in the farmyard," said Grandpa.

5 Little Critter thought, *If Little Sister were here, she would follow me on her tricycle.*

6 Little Critter got his bicycle out of the barn. His mom had hung his helmet on the handlebars.

7 "I can't go anywhere without my helmet!" said Little Critter.

8 Little Critter rode past the goats, the sheep, Grandma's garden, and the chicken coop. He rode around the back of the horse barn. Up ahead he saw a big rock in the path. Little Critter stopped. It wasn't a rock at all. It was a brown turtle with orange patterns on its back!

9 Little Critter did not want to scare the turtle back into his shell. He quietly watched the turtle crawl back into the grass. *Wow,* thought Little Critter. *That was a cool turtle. Little Sister would really have liked that turtle. I will have to tell her about it.*

Working with Words

Write a compound word for the underlined words in each sentence.

1. A <u>yard</u> that is part of a <u>farm</u> is a

   _____

2. A <u>storm</u> that brings <u>snow</u> is a

   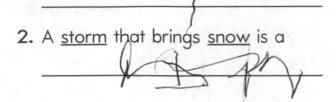

Write the best word to finish each sentence below.

3. Be sure to look over _____ answer. (each   ears)

4. Little Critter saw a _____ (turkey   turtle)

5. Little Critter rode his _____ (tricycle   bicycle)

6. _____ to do your best. (Try   Fry)

Reading and Thinking

1. Number the sentences to show what happened first, second, third, and last.

   _____ Little Critter wanted to go on a bike ride.

   _____ Little Critter saw a turtle.

   _____ Grandpa had to finish some chores.

   _____ Little Critter wanted to tell Little Sister about the turtle.

Write the best word to finish each sentence.

2. The child took the _____ puppy for a walk. (deep, little, helmet)

3. Can you see your _____ in the glass? (family, idea, face)

Look at the picture with the story. Write the best word to finish each sentence about the picture.

4. Little Critter has a _____ helmet. (red, blue, yellow)

5. There are _____ along the paths. (trees, roads, cars)

6. The farmyard is _____. (dirty, clean, moving)

119

A Letter from Little Sister

Read to see what Little Sister sends Little Critter.

1 When Little Critter came back from his bike ride, Grandma was making some sandwiches in the kitchen. "There's a letter here for you, Little Critter," she said.

2 "I got another letter?" asked Little Critter. The envelope felt heavy. *What could it be?* he thought. He opened it up and read it out loud.

3 Dear Little Critter,

Mom is helping me write a letter to you. It sounds like you are having fun on the farm. I was playing with some of your toys, but I put them away when I was done. I am sending you a picture that I drew.

Love,

Little Sister

4 Grandma said, "It sounds like your little sister misses you, Little Critter."

5 "I kind of miss her, too," said Little Critter, "except she always follows me around."

6 "That's because you're her big brother. She looks up to you," said Grandma.

7 Little Critter opened up the drawing that Little Sister had made. It was a picture of him with Little Sister. She wrote "Little Sister" and "Big Brother" in blue crayon next to each drawing.

8 "Let's hang that up here in the kitchen, so we can all enjoy it," said Grandma.

Knowing the Words

In each row, circle the two words with opposite meanings.

1. cool   cold   big   little
2. light   old   used   heavy

Working with Words

Walk and **talk** are rhyming words. In rhyming words, only the beginning sound is different. The missing words below rhyme with **shook**. Change **sh** in **shook** to **l**, **b**, **c**, and **t**. Then write each new word in the right sentence.

1. _____   3. _____
2. _____   4. _____

5. We _____ the wrong road.
6. Did you read the _____?
7. I can _____ dinner.
8. Did the car _____ new?

Write the best word to finish each sentence below.

9. I have not _____ her before. (send   seen)
10. We rode the _____ to school. (bone   bus)

Reading and Thinking

1. Check the answer that tells what the story is mostly about.
   _____ a picture of Little Sister
   _____ Grandma's sandwiches
   _____ a letter from Little Sister

Read these sentences. Then fill in the blanks.

2. Grandma cooked as she talked to Little Critter.
   She stands for _____.

3. Little Critter held the letter as he read it to Grandma.
   It stands for _____.

Write the best word to finish each sentence below.

4. The friends _____ letters at camp. (tell, write, do)
5. Some animals _____ berries. (make, buy, eat)
6. Did you _____ the milk? (stay, drink, grow)
7. Why do you think Little Sister was playing with Little Critter's toys?

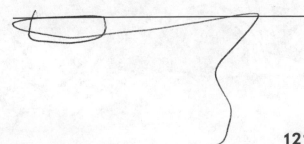

121

A Picnic for Dinner

Read to find out who would pack a healthier picnic.

1 "Grandma, are you making peanut butter and pickle sandwiches?" asked Little Critter.

2 "No, not today, Little Critter. These are chicken sandwiches. I thought we could go on a picnic for dinner tonight," said Grandma.

3 "A picnic! I love picnics!" said Little Critter.

4 Grandma and Grandpa and Little Critter walked to the apple orchard. There were rows and rows of trees filled with small green apples.

5 "Can we eat these apples, Grandma?" asked Little Critter.

6 "Not yet. They won't be ready until the fall," she said.

7 Grandpa spread out the picnic blanket. Grandma put the picnic basket on the blanket.

8 Grandma had packed chicken sandwiches, coleslaw, carrot sticks, strawberries, and some oatmeal cookies for dessert.

9 "Next time I can pack the picnic for you, Grandma," said Little Critter, "I'll bring brownies, potato chips, popcorn, cupcakes, and some soda pop. Oh yeah, and some peanut butter and pickle sandwiches."

10 Grandma and Grandpa grinned at each other.

11 "Don't you worry, Little Critter. Grandma is always glad to pack the picnic!" said Grandpa. "She has a knack for putting together a balanced meal."

12 "I sure do!" said Grandma. "Now eat your sandwich, Little Critter."

Knowing the Words

Circle the three words in each row that belong together.

1. apples   oranges   cats   bananas
2. chicken   dog   turkey   peacock
3. cookie   cake   candy   pizza
4. cake   water   milk   juice

Working with Words

Write the best word to finish each sentence below.

1. The class will _____ for the bird. (care   car)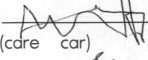

2. Did someone _____ dinner? (barn   burn)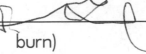

Most words add -**s** or -**es** to show more than one. Words that end in **y** are different. In most words that end in **y**, change the **y** to **i**, and add -**es**. Change the words below to mean more than one. One is done for you.

    berry   _berries_

3. story

4. penny

5. puppy

6. library

Reading and Thinking

1. Check the answer that tells what the story is mostly about.

    ____ a picnic

    ____ eating apples

    ____ peanut butter and pickle sandwiches

2. Why couldn't Little Critter eat the apples?

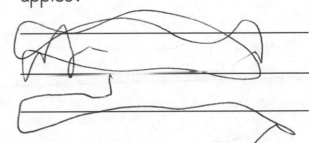

3. Why is Grandma's picnic a "balanced" meal?

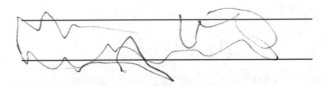

4. What would you pack for a healthy picnic?

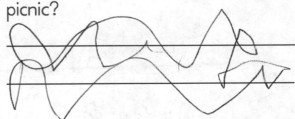

5. Check three answers that are healthy snacks.

    ____ potato chips

    ____ strawberries

    ____ carrot sticks

    ____ candy

    ____ raisins

Making a Scarecrow

Read to find out how Grandpa and Little Critter make a scarecrow.

1   After the picnic, Grandpa and Little Critter walked out to the cornfield. The cornstalks were taller than both of them. There were some large, black birds in the field eating the corn.

2   "Little Critter, I think we need to make a scarecrow," said Grandpa, "before these crows eat all of our corn."

3   "A scarecrow! That will be fun to make," said Little Critter.

4   Grandpa gathered some hay. Little Critter asked Grandma for some old clothes. They made the scarecrow's head by stuffing an old rag with hay and tying the bottom with some rope. Little Critter drew a face with a smile. They stuffed the rest of the clothes with hay and tied them together. They gave the scarecrow one of Grandpa's old fishing hats. Then they tied the scarecrow to a wooden pole.

5   "How does the scarecrow work, Grandpa?" asked Little Critter.

6   "We stand it up in the cornfield, Little Critter," said Grandpa. "Hopefully the crows will think it's a real critter and be too scared to come down," said Grandpa.

7   "Watch out, crows! This is the meanest, scariest scarecrow ever!" said Little Critter.

Knowing the Words

Write the words from the story that have these meanings.

1. black birds _____ (Par. 2)

2. not after _____ (Par. 2)

Working with Words

Circle the right word to finish the sentence. Then write the word in the blank.

1. I finished _____ grade.
   (first   forest)

2. You are too _____
   to reach the top. (sharp   short)

The letter **c** can stand for the sound of **s** as in **city** and **k** as in **cat**. Circle words that have **c** as in **city**. Cross out words that have a **c** as in **cat**.

city   ~~cat~~

3. crawl   cent   corn   scarecrow

4. across   place   tractor   ice

5. once   crow   dance   come

6. clown   bounce   popcorn   face

7. magic   princess   picnic   clothes

Reading and Thinking

1. Number the sentences to show what happened first, second, third, and last.

   ____ Grandpa and Little Critter made a scarecrow.

   ____ The crows were eating the corn.

   ____ Little Critter said, "Watch out crows!"

   ____ Grandpa gathered some hay.

2. What did Grandpa and Little Critter make the scarecrow out of?

   _____

   _____

3. Why did Grandpa want to make a scarecrow? _____

   _____

4. The crows are scared of a scarecrow because _____

   _____

5. Do you think the scarecrow will work? Why? _____

   _____

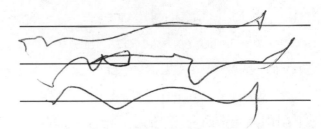

Fishing at the Pond

Read to see if Little Critter and Grandpa catch any fish.

1 "Can we go fishing now, Grandpa?" asked Little Critter.

2 "Yes, we can, Little Critter. All the chores are done for the day!" said Grandpa.

3 Grandpa and Little Critter headed for the pond with their fishing poles. They sat together on the creaky wooden dock. Crickets chirped and frogs croaked. Bright green dragonflies darted across the water. Grandpa showed Little Critter how to put a worm on the fishhook. "Be careful," said Grandpa, "the hook is sharp. Now, cast your line, like this." Grandpa flicked his fishing line into the middle of the pond.

4 When Little Critter tried, his line got caught on Grandpa's hat.

5 "Sorry, Grandpa," said Little Critter, as he reeled in the soggy hat.

6 "Try again, Little Critter," said Grandpa.

7 Little Critter cast his line into the pond again. "I know I'm going to catch the biggest fish in the pond," said Little Critter.

8 Hours later, Little Critter and Grandpa still had not caught anything. "Fishing takes some patience, doesn't it, Little Critter?" asked Grandpa.

9 "It sure does, but I think it's fun being here at the pond with you, Grandpa," said Little Critter.

Knowing the Words

Write the words from the story that have these meanings.

1. pointy _____
(Par. 3)

2. center _____
(Par. 3)

3. wet _____
(Par. 5)

Working with Words

A word part that can be said by itself is called a **syllable**. Some words have two consonants between two vowels. These words can be divided between the consonants, as in **pic|nic**. Write each word below. Then draw a line to divide the word into syllables.

1. little _____

2. soggy _____

3. middle _____

Circle the right word to finish each sentence. Then write the word in the blank.

4. Did you hear the _____?
   (knew, knock, know)

5. I knew that was the _____
   answer. (write, wrong, wrote)

Reading and Thinking

1. Number the sentences to show what happened first, second, third, and last.

   _____ All the chores were done.

   _____ Little Critter cast his line into the pond.

   _____ Grandpa and Little Critter went to the pond.

   _____ Grandpa's hat got wet.

2. What did Grandpa show Little Critter how to do?

   _____

   _____

   _____

3. Check two sentences that tell about the pond.

   _____ Sharks live there.

   _____ Frogs live there.

   _____ Fish live there.

   _____ There is no water.

Four Shiny Marbles

Read to find out what Little Critter can buy with a dollar.

1 "Little Critter, would you like to go into town today?" asked Grandpa.

2 "Sure, Grandpa!" said Little Critter.

3 Grandma gave Little Critter four shiny quarters. "Buy a treat, Little Critter," said Grandma.

4 "Thank you, Grandma!" said Little Critter. He put the quarters in his pocket.

5 In town, Grandpa said, "Let's go into the general store."

6 "What's the general store?" asked Little Critter.

7 "It's a place where you can buy anything and everything!" said Grandpa.

8 Little Critter wandered around the store. Should he spend his quarters on candy? Or a kite? Or a yo-yo? "Look at those marbles!" said Little Critter.

9 Little Critter felt the smooth, shiny marbles. The sign said 25 cents each. Little Critter asked Grandpa, "How many cents are in a quarter?"

10 "Twenty-five, Little Critter," said Grandpa. "You can buy one marble with each quarter."

11 "I can buy four marbles!" exclaimed Little Critter. He chose a speckled blue marble, a clear marble, an orange and green marble, and a bright red marble.

12 "That will be one dollar," said the store clerk.

13 "But I only have four quarters!" said Little Critter.

14 "That's just right," said Grandpa. "Four quarters is the same as one dollar!"

Reading and Thinking

1. Check the answer that tells what the story is mostly about.

   _____ buying a kite

   _____ buying some marbles

   _____ saving money

Write the best word to finish each sentence.

2. Please _____ before you answer.
   (carry, hide, think)

3. We ran _____ the house in the rain.
   (toward, over, away)

Look at the picture on this page. Answer these questions about it.

4. What else does the general store sell?

   _____

   _____

5. What is Little Critter doing?

   _____

Working with Words

The ending **-y** added to a word can mean "full of." The word **rainy** means "full of rain." Write the meanings for these words. One is done for you.

   dirty   _full of dirt_

1. grassy   _____

2. creamy   _____

In rhyming words, only the beginning sound is different. In each sentence, write the word from the box that rhymes with the underlined word.

soap	bright	caught

3. Late at <u>night</u>, the stars are very

   _____

4. I <u>hope</u> that I can find the

   _____

5. My mother <u>bought</u> the fish that I

   _____

Circle the right word to finish each sentence. Write the word in the blank.

6. We played, _____ we lost.
   (bit, bat, but)

7. Did you find your _____?
   (hit, hat, hot)

129

A Gift for Grandma and Grandpa

Read to find out what Little Critter gives Grandma and Grandpa.

1   Little Critter was sitting on the floor playing with his new marbles. Grandpa was taking a nap on the couch. Grandma was sewing.

2   "Does anyone want to play checkers?" asked Little Critter. Grandpa snored. Grandma said, "Maybe later."

3   Little Critter wandered upstairs. *Soon Mom and Dad and Little Sister will come get me. I will miss Grandma and Grandpa, but I will be glad to be home,* Little Critter thought.

4   Little Critter made a card for Grandma and Grandpa.

5   Dear Grandma and Grandpa,

I have had fun at the farm. I love the animals. The country fair was fun, too. I liked fishing with you, Grandpa, and baking pies with you, Grandma. I will miss you when I go home, but we can write letters. I am giving you a present, too.

Love,

Little Critter

6   Later, Little Critter gave his grandparents the card. "Thank you, Little Critter," said Grandma.

7   "We're going to miss you around here, Little Critter," said Grandpa.

8   "Close your eyes and put out your hand," said Little Critter.

9   Little Critter placed a red marble in Grandpa's hand and a blue marble in Grandma's hand.

10   "Thank you, Little Critter! These pretty marbles are a treasure," said Grandma. "We'll keep them right here in the kitchen window."

Reading and Thinking

1. Check the answer that tells what the story is mostly about.

   _____ crayons and paper

   _____ a present for Grandma and Grandpa

   _____ Grandpa's nap

2. Why did Little Critter go upstairs?

   _____

   _____

   _____

3. What did Little Critter give to Grandma and Grandpa?

   _____

   _____

4. Why do you think Grandma said the marbles were a treasure?

   _____

   _____

Working with Words

Fill in each blank with the right pair of letters to make a word.

ar   er   or

1. Will you read me a st____y?

2. We worked with flashc____ds.

3. She took h____ book home.

The letter **g** can stand for the sound of **j** as in **cage** and **g** as in **girl**. Circle words that have **g** as in **cage**. Cross out words that have g as in **girl**.

4. glad   large   hungry   goose

5. orange   get   tag   together

Write the compound words that can be made from the words below.

   sun   thing   shine   any

6. _____   7. _____

In each sentence, circle two words with the same vowel sound as the word in dark print.

8. **soap**   Wear your coat when you walk down the road.

9. **grow**   I can throw the ball low.

Pancake Breakfast

Read about what Little Critter wants for breakfast.

1   Little Critter was outside with Grandpa feeding the animals when Grandma called, "Breakfast is ready!"

2   Grandma put a tall stack of pancakes in front of Grandpa. She poured coffee for Grandpa and orange juice for Little Critter.

3   "I'm not that hungry, Grandma," said Little Critter.

4   "Not hungry?" asked Grandma. "I thought you'd like a special breakfast on your last day here."

5   "I'll just have some coffee like Grandpa," said Little Critter.

6   "I didn't know you drank coffee, Little Critter," said Grandma.

7   "Oh, yes, I like coffee," said Little Critter.

8   Grandma poured a little coffee into a mug for Little Critter. He took a small sip. Then he spit the bitter coffee out of his mouth into a napkin.

9   "I guess I don't like this kind," said Little Critter.

10   "I have something you will like better," said Grandma.

11   Grandma poured some pancake batter onto the hot griddle. Little Critter watched her flip some funny-shaped pancakes. Soon she gave him two pancakes, one shaped like a letter "L", and the other a "C".

12   " 'L' is for Little," said Grandma, "and C is for Critter. Especially for you."

13   Little Critter smiled as he put butter and maple syrup on his letters. "Thanks, Grandma. This *is* a special breakfast."

Reading and Thinking

1. Grandma made some funny

_____

for Little Critter.

2. What didn't Little Critter like?

_____

Write **T** if the sentence is true. Write **F** if it is not true.

3. _____ Little Critter likes coffee.

4. _____ Grandpa drinks coffee.

5. _____ Grandpa was eating eggs for breakfast.

6. Do you think Little Critter liked the pancakes? Why?

_____

_____

Working with Words

Circle words that have **c** as in **city**.
Cross out words that have **c** as in **cat**.

1. picture   uncle   bounce   nice

2. pancake   corner   face   cut

3. fence   across   candy   dance

An **'s** at the end of a word may be used to show that something belongs to someone. Change these groups of words using **'s**.

4. the pancake of Little Critter

_____ pancake

5. the coffee that belongs to Grandpa

_____ coffee

6. the breakfast of Grandma

_____ breakfast

Circle the right word to finish each sentence. Then write the word in the blank.

7. I can't _____ of it.
(think, thank, tent)

8. She _____ into the apple.
(bat, bit, but)

Little Sister Wants to Have Fun

Find out how Little Critter helps Little Sister have some fun.

1   When his family arrived, Little Critter told everyone about his visit. "I fed the pigs and the sheep. I rode a horse, and I helped bake a blackberry pie. I went to the general store and the country fair. I ate too much cherry pie at the fair and got a tummy ache. I know how to take care of goats and how to milk a cow."

2   "I'm glad you had a good time, Little Critter," said Mrs. Critter.

3   "I even beat Grandpa at checkers," said Little Critter.

4   "No fair!" said Little Sister. "You get to do everything just because you're bigger." She folded her arms and frowned.

5   "Do you want to go see the pond?" Little Critter asked his sister.

6   "No," said Little Sister.

7   "Do you want to go look for the turtle that I found?" he asked.

8   "No," she said.

9   Little Critter had another idea, "Want to play checkers?"

10   "Okay," said Little Sister.

11   Little Critter and Little Sister set up Grandpa's checkerboard. Little Sister said, "These checkers look like cookies!"

12   "Grandpa made them," said Little Critter.

13   Little Sister won three games in a row. "This is fun!" she said. "I guess you're a pretty good big brother."

Knowing the Words

Write the words from the story that have these meanings.

1. a game _____
   (Par. 3)

2. made a sad face _____
   (Par. 4)

Working with Words

Circle the right word. Write it in the blank.

1. Hold on to the _____ of the kite. (string   spring)

2. We planted a _____ in the yard. (tree   free)

3. Say the word **bake.** Listen to the vowel sound of the word. In each word below, circle the two letters that stand for that sound.

   afraid   stay   away   paint

The letter **g** can stand for the sound of **j** as in **cage** and **g** as in **girl.** Circle words that have **g** as in **girl.** Cross out words that have **g** as in **cage.**

   (girl)   ~~cage~~

4. general   village   big   bag
5. danger   goats   large   again
6. dog   strange   orange   game

Reading and Thinking

1. Why did Little Critter play checkers with Little Sister?

   _____

Write **T** if the sentence is true. Write **F** if it is not true.

2. _____ Little Critter was angry.

3. _____ Little Sister had fun playing checkers.

4. How did Little Sister feel after Little Critter played with her?

   _____

   _____

Saying Good-bye to the Farm

Read to find out why Little Critter won't be sad.

1   It was time for the Critter family to head home. Little Critter walked around the farmyard to say good-bye to all the animals. Little Sister followed him.

2   They went to the sheep pen first. "Good-bye, sheep!" said Little Critter. "Good-bye, sheep!" said Little Sister.

3   Then they went to the barn. "Good-bye, Old Kicker and Buttercup," said Little Critter. "Good-bye, Old Kicker and Buttercup," said Little Sister.

4   "*Next time* it will be your turn to visit the farm, Little Sister," said Little Critter.

5   "I can't wait until next time!" she said.

6   Little Critter hugged Grandma and Grandpa good-bye. He remembered his good manners. "Thank you for everything, Grandma and Grandpa."

7   "Don't look so sad, Little Critter," said Grandpa.

8   Mrs. Critter said, "I think I can cheer you up, Little Critter. What if Grandma and Grandpa come visit us in a couple of weeks?"

9   "That would be great! But, what about all the animals?" asked Little Critter.

10   "We have some kind friends who will feed our animals while we visit you," said Grandma.

11   "That's good," said Little Critter, "because I don't think we can fit all those animals in our house!"

Knowing the Words

Write the words from the story that have these meanings.

1. to go see someone

   _____
   (Par. 4)

2. did not forget

   _____
   (Par. 6)

Working with Words

Use these words to make compound words. Then use the compound words to finish each sentence below.

   every   farm   thing   yard

1. Thank you for _____.

2. The sheep live in the _____.

An **'s** at the end of a word may be used to show that something belongs to someone. Change these groups of words using **'s**.

3. the animals of Grandpa

   _____

4. the barn of the horse

   _____

5. the hat of mom

   _____

Reading and Thinking

1. Check the answer that tells what the story is mostly about.

   _____ following Little Critter
   _____ saying good-bye
   _____ talking to animals

2. What was Little Sister doing in the story? _____
   _____

3. Check the sentence that tells why Little Critter looked sad.

   _____ He was going to miss the farm.
   _____ He didn't like the animals.
   _____ Little Sister made him cry.

4. Who will take care of the animals when Grandma and Grandpa come for a visit? _____

5. Check the sentence that tells why Little Critter won't be sad.

   _____ He is going to live at the farm.
   _____ Little Sister gave him some money.
   _____ Grandma and Grandpa are coming for a visit soon.

6. How did Little Critter show his good manners? _____
   _____

Glad to Be Home

Read to see what Little Critter thinks when he wakes up at home.

1 When Little Critter got home, he went right to his room. He was glad to see his own bed. He was glad to see his football helmet, his skateboard, and his Super Critter costume. He put his two new marbles on the table next to his bed. They would remind him of the farm until he could visit again.

2 Mom and Dad came in. "Good night, Little Critter," said Mom. She gave him a hug.

3 "We're glad you are home," said his dad. "We missed you."

4 "I missed you, too," said Little Critter, as he climbed into his bed and turned out the light. His room at home was not too dark. It was just right. He dreamed about green and yellow cornfields and chasing furry little lambs. He dreamed about blackberry pie and letter-shaped pancakes.

5 The next morning when Little Critter woke up, he thought, *Oh, no! There are chores to do! I have to feed the animals! I'm late!* He looked around. He saw that he was home in his own room. He smiled and said, "I can sleep in today!" Little Critter pulled the blankets around him and went back to sleep.

Reading and Thinking

1. Number the sentences to show what happened first, second, third, and last.

_____ Little Critter's mom and dad said good night.

_____ Little Critter went back to sleep.

_____ Little Critter was glad to see his own room.

_____ Little Critter remembered he was at home.

2. Where did Little Critter think he was when he woke up?

_____

_____

Working with Words

Rewrite these words to mean more than one. Remember to change the **y** to **i** before adding **-es**.

1. country _____

2. city _____

3. family _____

4. Say the word **keep.** Listen to the vowel sound in the word. In each word below, circle the two letters that stand for that sound.

feet   each   seed   deep

The spelling of some base words is changed before an ending is added. Words such as **happy** must have the **y** changed to **i** before adding an ending. Endings are word parts like **-er, -est,** and **-ed.** Change the **y** to **i** and add the endings to these words. One is done for you.

carry   +   ed   ___*carried*___

5. heavy   +   est   _____

6. hurry   +   ed   _____

7. merry   +   er   _____

8. hungry   +   est   _____

Knowing the Words

Write the story words that have these meanings.

1. a tool that scoops
   shovel
   (Par. 1)

2. place where plants grow
   garden
   (Par. 5)

3. taught
   trained
   (Par. 7)

Reading and Thinking

1. This story is mostly about
   ___ Little Critter's room.
   ✓ a problem with Blue.
   ___ a problem with Little Sister.

Words such as **he**, **she**, and **it** take the place of other words. Read these sentences. Then fill in the blanks.

1. Little Critter shouted as he ran.
   He stands for _Little Critter_

2. Her mom laughed as she talked.
   She stands for _her mom_

3. My dad talked as he worked.
   He stands for _my dad_

5

Reading and Thinking

Put each word in the right blank.
dig   garden   inside

1. Little Critter helped fix the _garden_

2. Blue likes to _dig_

3. Little Critter sat _inside_ the doghouse.

Circle the right answer.
4. What does Little Critter want Blue to do?
   stay in the doghouse
   (stop digging)
   water the garden

5. What did Little Critter tell Blue?
   to stop digging (accept other
   similar answers)

Working with Words

Circle the best word for each sentence. Then write it in the blank.

1. Little Critter and Blue _sat_ in the doghouse.
   (sat)   can   cat

2. Blue likes to _dig_ in the garden.
   dog   (dig)   dug

3. Little Critter will _train_ Blue.
   trap   rain   (train)

7

Knowing the Words

Write the story words that have these meanings.

1. place for mail
   mailbox
   (Par. 2)

2. ran after
   chased
   (Par. 3)

3. made an unhappy face
   frowned
   (Par. 6)

Reading and Thinking

1. What is the name of Little Critter's neighbor?
   Mrs. Crabtree

   Why do you think she was frowning?
   Answers will vary. Example:
   Because Blue ran in her yard.

2. What happened first in the story? Put **1** by it. What happened next? Put **2** by it. Put **3** by the thing that happened last.

   _2_ Little Critter chased Blue.

   _3_ Little Critter ran into Mrs. Crabtree.

   _1_ Little Critter went to get the mail.

9

Reading and Thinking

1. What did Blue do? _He dug up_
   Mrs. Crabtree's roses.

2. How did Blue show he was sorry?
   He put his head on the
   ground.

3. Why did Little Critter want to check his piggy bank? _He wanted to_
   see how much money he had.

Working with Words

Circle the best word for each sentence. Then write it in the blank.

1. Little Critter will _pay_ for the roses.
   day   say   (pay)

2. _Thank_ you for the new toy.
   Bank   (Thank)   Think

3. Blue put his head on the _ground_
   grow   grind   (ground)

4. Little Critter walked _home_ with Blue.
   hope   hum   (home)

11

140

Knowing the Words

Write the story words that have these meanings.

1. people you like a lot

   <u>friends</u>
   (Par. 1)

2. crushed or wrinkled

   <u>crumpled</u>
   (Par. 3)

Circle the three words in each line that belong together.

3. (house) book (park) (store)
4. (bark) fly (howl) (jump)
5. soup (lunch) (dinner) (breakfast)
6. ball (friend) (neighbor) (aunt)

Reading and Thinking

1. This story is mostly about
   ___ how Blue caused trouble.
   ✓ how Little Critter's friends help.
   ___ how Blue earns money.

2. Why does Little Critter need more money?
   <u>He does not have enough</u>
   <u>to pay for the roses.</u>

3. Can you think of a way for Little Critter to earn money?
   <u>Answers will vary.</u>

13

Reading and Thinking

Some of these sentences are about **real** things, things that could happen. Write **R** by them. The other sentences are about things that could not happen, **make-believe** things. Write **M** by them.

1. <u>R</u> A dog can run and play.
2. <u>M</u> A house can talk.
3. <u>R</u> A dog likes bones.
4. <u>M</u> A dog likes to read.
5. What was Gabby's idea? <u>to sell</u>
   <u>lemonade</u>

Learning to Study

Write each set of words in A-B-C order.

1. cups   table   lemonade
   <u>cups</u>
   <u>lemonade</u>
   <u>table</u>

2. chairs   idea   house
   <u>chairs</u>
   <u>house</u>
   <u>idea</u>

3. later   sign   money
   <u>later</u>
   <u>money</u>
   <u>sign</u>

15

Reading and Thinking

Put each word in the right blank.

   walked   pulled   sniffed

1. Blue <u>sniffed</u> Fifi.
2. Su Su <u>walked</u> with Fifi.
3. Fifi <u>pulled</u> on the leash.

Write **R** by the sentences that are about **real** things. Write **M** by the sentences about **make-believe** things.

4. <u>M</u> Dogs can make lemonade.
5. <u>R</u> People can make lemonade.
6. <u>R</u> People put ice in lemonade.
7. <u>M</u> Ice keeps drinks warm.

Working with Words

A **base** word is a word without an ending. The words in each row have the same **base** word. Circle the ending of each one. Then write the **base** word in the blank.

1. play(ing)
   play(ed)
   play(s)
   <u>play</u>

2. start(ing)
   start(ed)
   start(s)
   <u>start</u>

Circle the best word for each sentence. Then write it in the blank.

3. We'll eat <u>when</u> he comes.
   then   (when)   check

4. Please finish <u>those</u> apples.
   chase   (those)   shoes

17

Reading and Thinking

1. What did Mrs. Smith say about the lemonade? <u>She said it was</u>
   <u>tasty.</u>

2. Why was Little Critter proud?
   <u>Because Mrs. Smith bought</u>
   <u>two cups of lemonade.</u>

3. Write **1**, **2**, and **3** by these sentences to show what happened first, next, and last.
   <u>2</u> Mrs. Smith bought lemonade.
   <u>1</u> Little Sister came outside.
   <u>3</u> Tiger put the nickels in the cup.

Learning to Study

Write each set of words in A-B-C order.

1. that   day   outside
   <u>day</u>
   <u>outside</u>
   <u>that</u>

2. nickels   customer   jingled
   <u>customer</u>
   <u>jingled</u>
   <u>nickels</u>

3. tasty   muddy   dollars
   <u>dollars</u>
   <u>muddy</u>
   <u>tasty</u>

19

141

Page 21

Write the story words that have these meanings.

1. paid money for

   bought
   (Par. 1)

2. make higher

   raise
   (Par. 5)

3. the next day

   tomorrow
   (Par. 9)

Put a check by the meaning that fits the underlined word in each sentence.

4. Is it <u>hard</u> to make new friends?

   ___ something not soft

   ✓ something not easy to do

5. I will <u>watch</u> Blue play.

   ___ thing that tells time

   ✓ look at

1. How much money was in the cup?

   45 cents

2. This story is mostly about

   ___ why Little Critter needs money.

   ___ selling a lot of lemonade.

   ✓ a slow day at the lemonade stand.

3. Why did Little Sister say to raise the price? Because they needed a lot more money.

4. What did Tiger say to do? Tiger said to go into town tomorrow.

21

Page 23

1. This story is mostly about

   ✓ Gabby's idea.

   ___ Gabby's dog.

   ___ Blue's paws.

2. Gabby wants to train Blue for the show because first prize is twenty-five dollars

3. Do you think that Gabby can train Blue? Answers will vary.

Circle the best word for each sentence. Then write it in the blank.

1. I want to read this ___ book

   boat   back   (book)

2. We will ___ work ___ hard.

   (work)   walk   week

Write -ing or -ed in each blank.

3. I talk ___ ed ___ with her yesterday.

4. She want ___ ed ___ to work.

5. Now she is train ___ ing ___ Blue.

Circle the right word for each sentence. Then write it in the blank.

6. Tiger is my best ___ friend

   ground   proud   (friend)

7. I need a ___ drink ___ of water.

   trick   (drink)   break

23

Page 25

Look at each picture and circle the sentence that goes with it.

1. (Blue is playing outside.)

   Blue is playing in the house.

2. Blue sleeps on Little Critter's bed.

   (Blue sleeps in his doghouse.)

3. What did Mr. Critter say about the dog show? He said it was a good idea.

4. What will Little Critter do if Blue wins the dog show? Little Critter will pay Mrs. Crabtree.

5. What did Little Sister say about Blue? She said Blue has a lot to learn.

Circle the best word for each sentence. Then write it in the blank.

1. Blue has a ___ tail

   tan   than   (tail)

2. Blue can win a ___ prize

   (prize)   quiet   paint

3. The floor was ___ wet

   pet   met   (wet)

Write these sentences. Use one of the shorter words from the box to stand for the words that are underlined.

We'll	isn't	can't	didn't	I'm

4. <u>We will</u> be there.

   We'll be there.

5. He <u>did not</u> go.

   He didn't go.

6. The puppy <u>is not</u> hurt.

   The puppy isn't hurt.

7. <u>I am</u> hungry.

   I'm hungry.

8. Blue <u>cannot</u> do tricks.

   Blue can't do tricks.

25

Page 27

1. This story is mostly about

   ___ Tiger's ball.

   ___ Gabby's dog.

   ✓ Blue's first lesson.

Fill in the blanks.

2. Little Critter said, "good dog," as he petted Blue.

   He stands for ___ Little Critter

3. Gabby brought her book and put it on the table.

   It stands for ___ her book

Circle the best word for each sentence. Then write it in the blank.

1. The lesson is too ___ long

   leg   (long)   log

2. The dog's eyes are ___ big

   (big)   bag   buy

3. Gabby told Blue to ___ sit

   sat   set   (sit)

4. They have a ___ new ___ pet.

   now   not   (new)

Read these words and look at the pictures.

Gabby's friend   her friend's hand

You can see that you add **'s** when you want to show that the hand belongs to Little Critter. Now write these names the same way.

5. Little Critter Little Critter's hand

6. Gabby ___ Gabby's ___ hand

27

142

Knowing the Words

Write the story words that have these meanings.

1. ripped ___torn___ (Par. 2)
2. tapping sound ___knock___ (Par. 4)
3. set to go ___ready___ (Par. 4)

Circle the three words in each line that belong together.

4. (arms) flowers (feet) (hands)
5. (eyes) (ears) bag (mouth)
6. hair (brown) (white) (black)

Reading and Thinking

1. This story is mostly about
   ___ the next dog lesson.
   ✓ Blue eating too much.
   ___ a new kind of dog food.

2. How do you think Blue feels?
   ___Answers may include:___
   ___sick, tired, full, sad.___

3. What do you think Little Critter can do so this won't happen again?
   ___Answers will vary.___

29

Reading and Thinking

Put each word in the right blank.

read   learn   better

1. Blue felt much ___better___
2. Blue will ___learn___
3. Gabby ___read___ her book.
4. Write 1, 2, and 3 by these sentences to show what happened first, next, and last.
   1 The friends went to the park.
   3 Little Critter got tangled up.
   2 Blue wanted to play.

31

Working with Words

Circle the best word for each sentence. Then write it in the blank.

1. Can you read this ___book___?
   cook   look   (book)

2. Gabby ___met___ Little Critter today.
   mail   (met)   mean

3. Blue wanted to ___chew___ on his bone.
   shoe   (chew)   threw

The missing word in each sentence sounds like **right**. Change the **r** in **right** to **f, l,** or **n**. Write the new words. The first one is done.

4. _fight_   ___light___   ___night___

Use the words you made in sentences.

5. Please turn off the ___light___
6. We will not ___fight___ over the toys.
7. It rained last ___night___

Knowing the Words

Write the story words that have these meanings.

1. soft shoe
   ___slipper___ (Par. 1)

2. place to keep clothes
   ___closet___ (Par. 2)

Circle the three words in each line that belong together.

3. (walk) look (trot) (run)
4. (head) (tail) trick (feet)
5. (good) mean (great) (wonderful)

Reading and Thinking

1. This story is mostly about
   ✓ the missing slipper.
   ___ Blue's doghouse.
   ___ breakfast.

2. List three places Little Critter looked for the slipper.
   ___Answers may include: in the___
   ___toy box, under the sofa, in the___
   ___cupboards, in Little Sister's___
   ___closet, or in the doghouse.___

3. Where did Little Critter find the slipper? ___He found it in the___
   ___doghouse.___

4. What did Blue do to the slipper?
   ___Blue chewed the slipper.___

33

Reading and Thinking

1. This story is mostly about
   ___ Mrs. Crabtree's roses.
   ✓ Mrs. Crabtree's visit.
   ___ Mrs. Crabtree's feet.

2. Instead of sitting, Blue ___rolled___
   ___around in the grass.___

3. Why do you think Mrs. Crabtree came over? ___Answers will vary.___

Working with Words

Circle the best word for each sentence. Then write it in the blank.

1. Mrs. Crabtree ___came___ over.
   stayed   (came)   ate

2. I see you ___here___ every day.
   her   help   (here)

3. I ___like___ to brush my dog.
   little   (like)   let

Read these words and look at the pictures.

dog   dogs

You can see that you add **s** to show that you mean more than one dog. Write these words so that they mean more than one.

4. rose ___roses___
5. friend ___friends___
6. lesson ___lessons___

35

Reading and Thinking

Put each word in the right blank.

howl   smart   clapped

1. Fifi is so **smart**
2. Blue began to **howl**
3. Maurice and Molly **clapped**
4. What was Fifi wearing?
   She was wearing a new
   collar and a pink sweater.
5. How do you know Su Su didn't like the howling sound?
   Su Su covered her ears.
6. This story is mostly about
   ___ Fifi's new collar.
   ✓ Fifi and Blue's trick.
   ___ Little Sister's trick.

Learning to Study

Write each set of words in A-B-C order.

1. pink   sing   howl
   howl
   pink
   sing
2. stay   ears   yap
   ears
   stay
   yap
3. collar   trick   one
   collar
   one
   trick

Reading and Thinking

Put each word in the right blank.

Suddenly   bumped   wobbled

1. Blue **wobbled** from side to side.
2. **Suddenly**, the family heard a crash.
3. Blue **bumped** into the chair.
4. Why do you think Blue was chasing his own tail? Answers will vary.

Working with Words

Circle the best word for each sentence. Then write it in the blank.

1. Blue has a **long** tail.
   log   lost   (long)
2. We will **take** a walk.
   talk   (take)   tail

The missing word in each sentence sounds like **make**. Change the m in **make** to **b**, **t**, or **w**. Write the new words.

3. **bake**   **take**   **wake**

Use the words you made in sentences.

4. May we **take** a walk?
5. I like to **bake** cookies.
6. Did Blue **wake** you?

You know that **Mom's hand** means "the hand of Mom." Add **'s** when you write these names to show what belongs to each.

7. Dad **Dad's** coat
8. Tiger **Tiger's** baseball
9. Blue **Blue's** teeth

Knowing the Words

Write the story words that have these meanings.

1. complained
   grumbled
   (Par. 1)

2. not on top of
   under
   (Par. 3)

Put a check by the meaning that fits the underlined word in each sentence.

3. Blue will never act <u>right</u>.
   ✓ correctly
   ___ not left

4. Will Dad <u>play</u> with Blue?
   ✓ have fun
   ___ a show

Reading and Thinking

1. How did Little Critter feel?
   Answers may include: sad,
   grumpy, angry, blue.
2. Who helped Little Critter feel better?
   His mom helped him feel
   better.

Write **R** by the sentences that are about **real** things. Write **M** by the sentences that are about **make-believe** things.

3. **R** People can make beds.
4. **M** Dogs can make beds.
5. **M** A cat wears pajamas.
6. **R** A person wears pajamas.

Reading and Thinking

Put each word in the right blank.

cooked   family   ready

1. Dad **cooked** on the grill.
2. Who is **ready** for a hot dog?
3. Gabby's **family** came to the picnic.

Write **R** by the sentences that are about **real** things. Write **M** by the sentences about **make-believe** things.

4. **M** A hot dog can walk.
5. **R** A dog can walk.
6. **R** Birds can fly.
7. **M** Dogs can fly.

Working with Words

Circle the best word for each sentence. Then write it in the blank.

1. She likes to **pick** flowers.
   pet   pan   (pick)
2. Sit **back** and read.
   (back)   bake   best
3. I like **that** book.
   think   thank   (that)

Fill in the missing vowel (**i**, **o**, or **u**) so the sentence makes sense.

4. Write on the l**i**ne.
5. Please give Blue a b**o**ne.
6. May Blue **u**se this bowl?

Fill in each blank with **str** or **spr** so the sentence makes sense.

7. Here is a ball of **str**ing.
8. I will **spr**ay water on the grass.
9. Don't walk in the **str**eet.

Reading and Thinking

Put each word in the right blank.

shake   piece   Reward

1. __Reward__ Blue with a hot dog.

2. Blue ate a __piece__ of the hot dog.

3. Did Blue learn to __shake__ ?

Fill in the blanks.

4. Blue held out his paw, and Little Critter shook it.

It stands for __his paw__ .

5. Gabby and Mr. Critter were happy because they were helping.

They stands for __Gabby__ and __Mr. Critter__ .

6. Blue was carrying a bone as he ran.

He stands for __Blue__ .

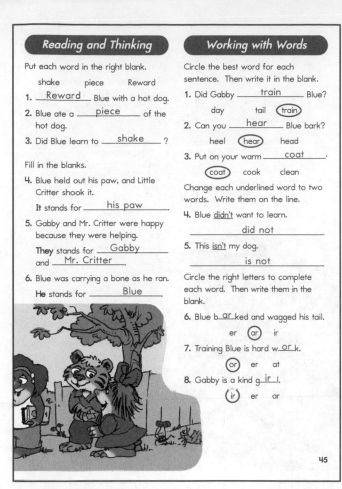

45

Working with Words

Circle the best word for each sentence. Then write it in the blank.

1. Did Gabby __train__ Blue?

day   tail   (train)

2. Can you __hear__ Blue bark?

heel   (hear)   head

3. Put on your warm __coat__ .

(coat)   cook   clean

Change each underlined word to two words. Write them on the line.

4. Blue didn't want to learn.

__did not__

5. This isn't my dog.

__is not__

Circle the right letters to complete each word. Then write them in the blank.

6. Blue b__ar__ked and wagged his tail.

er   (ar)   ir

7. Training Blue is hard w__or__k.

(or)   er   at

8. Gabby is a kind g__ir__l.

(ir)   er   ar

Knowing the Words

Write the story words that have these meanings.

1. meal at noon

__lunch__
(Par. 3)

2. someone who lives nearby

__neighbor__
(Par. 6)

3. well-known

__famous__
(Par. 10)

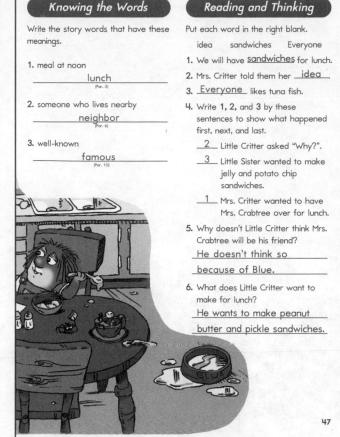

47

Reading and Thinking

Put each word in the right blank.

idea   sandwiches   Everyone

1. We will have __sandwiches__ for lunch.

2. Mrs. Critter told them her __idea__ .

3. __Everyone__ likes tuna fish.

4. Write 1, 2, and 3 by these sentences to show what happened first, next, and last.

__2__ Little Critter asked "Why?".

__3__ Little Sister wanted to make jelly and potato chip sandwiches.

__1__ Mrs. Critter wanted to have Mrs. Crabtree over for lunch.

5. Why doesn't Little Critter think Mrs. Crabtree will be his friend?

__He doesn't think so__ __because of Blue.__

6. What does Little Critter want to make for lunch?

__He wants to make peanut__ __butter and pickle sandwiches.__

Reading and Thinking

1. What did Blue bring to Mrs. Crabtree? __Answers may include: a doll,__ __pajamas, a baseball glove, a__ __teddy bear, or a towel.__

2. Why did Blue bring things to Mrs. Crabtree? __He was trying to be__ __her friend.__

3. Do you think Mrs. Crabtree likes Blue now? __Answers will vary.__

49

Working with Words

Read each sentence and circle the word that is made of two shorter words. Write the two words on the lines.

1. (Someone) ate all the potato chips.

__Some__ __one__

2. Blue made (everyone) laugh.

__every__ __one__

3. Where is the (baseball) glove?

__base__ __ball__

Circle the best word for each sentence. Then write it in the blank.

4. Please __show__ us a trick.

who   (show)   those

5. Where are your __shoes__ ?

this   who's   (shoes)

6. Blue will __chase__ me.

shook   (chase)   shout

Reading and Thinking

Look at each picture and circle the sentence that goes with it.

1. (Blue likes to dig.)

Blue does not like to dig.

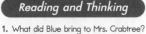

2. A mother can work.

(A mother can read.)

3. (He loves Blue.)

He doesn't like Blue.

4. What were Little Critter and Little Sister doing? __They were__ __watching a dog show on TV.__

5. What did Little Critter imagine? __He imagined that Blue won__ __the dog show.__

Working with Words

Write these sentences. Use one shorter word for the two words that are underlined.

1. She does not know my name.

__She doesn't know my__ __name.__

2. Blue will not sit.

__Blue won't sit.__

3. It is a beautiful day.

__It's a beautiful day.__

4. I am glad today.

__I'm glad today.__

Write these words so they mean more than one. One is done for you.

house __houses__

5. ribbon __ribbons__

6. doll __dolls__

7. window __windows__

51

145

Page 53

Knowing the Words

Write the story words that have these meanings.

1. wishing for ___hopeful___
   (Par. 1)

2. something worn on the neck
   ___scarf___
   (Par. 2)

3. ended ___finished___
   (Par. 6)

Put a check by the meaning that fits the underlined word in each sentence.

4. Blue <u>can</u> learn his lessons.
   ___ a thing to hold food
   ✓ knows how to

5. I must <u>check</u> for the mail.
   ___ make a line
   ✓ look with care

Reading and Thinking

1. Why was Little Sister mad?
   She was mad because
   Su Su made fun of Blue.

2. Do you think Su Su's dog will win?
   Answers will vary.

   Why or why not?
   Answers will vary.

3. Write 1, 2, and 3 by these sentences to show what happened first, next, and last.

   _2_ Little Sister got mad.
   _3_ Blue jumped on Little Sister.
   _1_ Su Su and Fifi walked by.

53

Page 55

Reading and Thinking

1. What was the surprise for Blue?
   The surprise was a new
   collar.

Put each word in the right blank.
   surprise   collar   wear

2. Mr. and Mrs. Critter had a
   ___surprise___ for Blue.

3. Blue got a new blue ___collar___

4. Blue will ___wear___ his new collar.

Working with Words

The missing word in each sentence sounds like **stop**. Change the **st** in **stop** to **t, m,** or **p**. Write the new words and put them in the right sentences.

1. _top_   _mop_   _pop_

2. Some popcorn didn't ___pop___

3. I hit the ___top___ of my head.

4. Clean the floor with a ___mop___

Circle the right letters for each sentence. Then write them in the blank.

5. They walked in the p_ar_k.
   er   ir   (ar)

6. What happened f_ir_st?
   ar   or   (ir)

Add **'s** to these words to show what belongs to each one.

7. dog   the ___dog's___ collar
8. cat   the ___cat's___ head
9. bird   the ___bird's___ nest
10. kitten the ___kitten's___ ball

55

Page 57

Knowing the Words

Write the story words that have these meanings.

1. place to keep a car ___garage___
   (Par. 2)

2. went after ___followed___
   (Par. 3)

Circle the three words in each line that belong together.

3. (paws) (tail) soft (head)

4. (glad) (happy) (pleased) sad

5. paint (grass) (park) (yard)

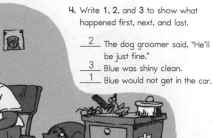

Reading and Thinking

1. This story is mostly about
   ___ Blue's visit to the vet.
   ✓ Blue's visit to the dog groomer.
   ___ Blue's visit to the pet store.

2. Why did the Critter family take Blue to be groomed? They took him
   to be groomed because the
   dog show was the next day.

3. What did Blue look like afterward?
   Blue was clean and his fur
   was cut short.

4. Write 1, 2, and 3 to show what happened first, next, and last.

   _2_ The dog groomer said, "He'll be just fine."
   _3_ Blue was shiny clean.
   _1_ Blue would not get in the car.

57

Page 59

Reading and Thinking

1. What did Blue do when he got out of the car?
   He raced to the garden.

2. What did Little Critter say to Blue?
   Little Critter said he wished
   Blue could stay clean.

Put each word in the right blank.
   splashed   carried   shampoo

3. Little Critter and Little Sister ___carried___ Blue upstairs.

4. They washed Blue with ___shampoo___

5. Blue ___splashed___ in the tub.

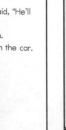

Working with Words

Fill in the missing vowel (**a, i,** or **o**) so each sentence makes sense.

1. You did a f_i_ne job.

2. Wash off with the h_o_se.

3. We will m_a_ke the bed.

Use the underlined words to make a new word to finish each sentence.

4. A <u>tub</u> that you take a <u>bath</u> in is called a ___bathtub___

5. A <u>yard</u> that is in <u>back</u> of a house is called a ___backyard___

Circle the best word for each sentence. Then write it in the blank.

6. Do not ___shout___ at me.
   show   (shout)   chair

7. Our dog is ___clean___
   boat   (clean)   stay

59

146

Put each word in the right blank.

collar   clapped   brought

1. Little Critter put a new **collar** on Blue.

2. Maurice and Molly **brought** hot dogs.

3. Everyone **clapped** for Scout.

4. This story is mostly about

   ✓ what the dogs do at the dog show.

   ___ what Tiger does at the dog show.

   ___ what Little Sister does at the dog show.

To make a word mean more than one, add **-es** if the word ends in **s, ss, ch, sh,** or **x.** Write these words so that they mean more than one.

1. lunch   **lunches**

2. dish   **dishes**

3. box   **boxes**

Fill in the missing letter so the sentence makes sense.

4. I like to h **e** lp my dad.

5. Blue j **u** mped on Little Critter.

6. Little Critter p **a** cked up the ball.

Fill in the missing letters so each sentence makes sense.

   ar   or   ur

7. Soon it will be Blue's t **ur** n.

8. Can we play in the p **ar** k?

61

Write the story words that have these meanings.

1. area for a show

   ring
   (Par. 1)

2. rope to hold an animal

   leash
   (Par. 3)

3. without warning

   suddenly
   (Par. 3)

4. tugged

   pulled
   (Par. 3)

5. to smell

   sniff
   (Par. 3)

Circle the three words in each line that belong together.

6. (sit) (heel) happy (shake)

7. (chair) (table) mail (rug)

8. box (brush) (broom) (mop)

9. (ran) sat (raced) (chased)

1. Who opened the box?
   One of the judges opened it.

2. Why was Blue a hero?
   Blue was a hero because he found stolen coins.

Look at each picture and circle the sentence that goes with it.

3. (Blue is digging a hole.)

   Blue is opening the box.

4. (Little Critter is happy.)

   Little Critter is angry.

63

1. What was special about the coins Blue found?
   They were from the Great Critterville Bank Robbery.

2. What did the bank do?
   The bank gave Little Critter a reward.

3. Write **1, 2,** and **3** to show what happened first, next, and last.

   _1_ Blue was a hero.

   _3_ Little Sister said she knew Blue would be famous.

   _2_ People from the newspaper came to see Little Critter.

In each row, circle the two letters in each word that make the same sound you hear in the underlined word.

   toy   po(i)nt   b(oy)   n(oi)se

1. show   kn(ow)   (ow)n   thr(ow)

2. see   tr(ee)   w(ee)ks   pl(ea)se

3. found   d(ow)n   ar(ou)nd   pr(ou)d

4. mean   n(ee)d   n(ea)t   r(ea)d

Circle the best word for each sentence. Then write it in the blank.

5. Do you like to play this **game**?
   same   (game)   name

6. Little Critter found **his** sister.
   hit   him   (his)

7. This is my **best** trick.
   (best)   nest   last

8. Little Sister hit the **ball**.
   (ball)   call   tell

Circle each **c** that stands for the sound of **s** in these words.

9. on(c)e   12. pie(c)e

10. doctor   13. be(c)ause

11. fen(c)e   14. come

65

Write the story words that have these meanings.

1. celebration

   party
   (Par. 1)

2. look for

   search
   (Par. 3)

3. the next day

   tomorrow
   (Par. 4)

Circle the three words in each line that belong together.

4. (heel) (sit) (stay) found

5. (collar) (leash) (tag) bird

6. hat (walk) (run) (stay)

7. mail (cake) (ice cream) (hot dogs)

Look at each picture and circle the sentence that goes with it.

1. Blue and Fifi do not like each other.

   (Blue and Fifi are friends.)

2. (Tiger likes hot dogs.)

   Tiger does not like hot dogs.

3. Why do you think Mrs. Crabtree wants to speak with the friends?
   Answers will vary.

4. Who gave Blue a medal?
   The Mayor of Critterville gave Blue a medal.

67

Reading and Thinking

1. This story is mostly about
   - ✓ how Mrs. Crabtree solves the problem.
   - ___ how the friends make more money.
   - ___ how Mrs. Critter solves the problem.

2. How did Little Critter pay Mrs. Crabtree back?
   Little Critter helped her plant new roses.

3. List three things the friends did for Mrs. Crabtree.
   Answers may include: The friends planted roses, pulled weeds, painted the fence, and swept the sidewalk and porch.

Working with Words

Circle the right letters for each sentence. Then write them in the blank.

1. Do you w_or_k hard?
   ar   (or)   ir

2. It is your t_ur_n to play.
   ar   or   (ur)

3. They will help plant the g_ar_den.
   er   or   (ar)

Circle the best word for each sentence. Then write it in the blank.

4. Can you make your __bed__?
   bag   (bed)   big

5. Gabby wrote a __letter__.
   listen   last   (letter)

6. We filled the __pan__ with milk.
   (pan)   pet   pop

Use the underlined words to make a new word to finish each sentence.

7. A house for a dog is called a __doghouse__.

8. A walk on the side of the street is called a __sidewalk__.

69

Reading and Thinking

1. What did Little Critter say to Blue?
   He said that Blue was the best dog in the world.

Fill in the blanks.

2. Tiger and Gabby talked as they worked.
   They stands for Tiger and Gabby

3. Mrs. Crabtree answered, and she said, "Yes, Little Critter."
   She stands for __Mrs. Crabtree__

Working with Words

The missing word in each sentence sounds like **new**. Change the n in **new** to **bl**, **fl**, and **thr**. Write the new words, and put them in the right sentences.

1. __blew__   __flew__   __threw__

2. The wind __blew__ hard.

3. I __threw__ my dog a ball.

4. The bird __flew__ away.

Circle the best word for each sentence. Then write it in the blank.

5. Little Critter will __brush__ Blue.
   grass   (brush)   growl

6. Will Maurice and Molly __play__ with us?
   dry   (play)   fry

The ending **-er** means "more" and the ending **-est** means "most." Add the endings **-er** and **-est** to these base words.

	-er	-est
clean	*cleaner*	*cleanest*
7. kind	kinder	kindest
8. fast	faster	fastest

71

Knowing the Words

Write the words from the story that have these meanings.

1. at night __evening__
   (Par. 1)

2. put things in a bag __pack__
   (Par. 4)

3. didn't remember __forgot__
   (Par. 8)

Working with Words

Circle the right word to finish the sentence. Then write the word in the blank.

1. The team ran a good __race__.
   (face, case, (race))

2. Hit the ball with the __bat__.
   (bell, (bat), bed)

Reading and Thinking

1. Check the answer that tells what the story is mostly about.
   - ___ good manners
   - ✓ packing for a trip
   - ___ riding a bicycle

2. Look at the picture. Check the two sentences that tell about the picture.

   - ✓ Little Critter is packing.
   - ✓ Little Critter has cowboy boots.
   - ___ Little Critter rides a bicycle.

3. Little Critter found a __bag__ to pack.

Some things are real and some are make-believe. Write **R** by real things. Write **M** by make-believe things.

4. __M__ Teddy bears can talk.
5. __R__ Children can learn.
6. __M__ Skateboards can write.

73

Knowing the Words

Write the words from the story that have these meanings.

1. thing you like best __favorite__
   (Par. 1)

2. to take __bring__
   (Par. 1)

3. must have __need__
   (Par. 2)

The words **come** and **go** have meanings so different that they are **opposite**. Make a line from each word in the first list to the word in the second list with the opposite meaning.

4. early — front
5. long ✗ short
6. back — late

Working with Words

A word without any ending is a **base word**. The base word of **talking** is **talk**. Circle each base word below.

1. (pick)s   2. (help)ed   3. (play)ing

Sometimes one word stands for two words. The word **didn't** stands for **did not**. Write a word from the story that can stand for each pair of words.

4. do not __don't__
   (Par. 4)

5. it is __it's__
   (Par. 7)

Reading and Thinking

1. Check the answer that tells what the story is mostly about.
   - ___ Little Critter's teddy bear
   - ✓ what Little Critter will do at the farm
   - ___ Little Sister's bicycle

2. What did Mrs. Critter help Little Critter do? She helped him pack his bag.

3. Check the sentence that tells what Little Sister wanted.
   - ___ to play checkers
   - ___ to go fishing
   - ✓ to go to the farm

4. Why did Mrs. Critter say Little Critter would not need his football helmet and skateboard?
   Little Critter would not be able to use those things at the farm.

75

Panel 1 (page 77)

Write the words from the story that have these meanings.

1. one more time ___again___
(Par. 4)

2. in a happy way ___cheerfully___
(Par. 7)

3. top part of the arm ___shoulder___
(Par. 7)

Circle the three words in each row that belong together.

4. (morning) year (night) (afternoon)
5. (coats) (hats) feet (shoes)
6. wet (cold) (warm) (hot)
7. (happy) (sad) (angry) old

Learning to Study

Number the words to show A-B-C order for each list.

1. _3_ morning　　2. _1_ farm
　 _4_ stop　　　　 _3_ soon
　 _2_ gas　　　　　_4_ took
　 _1_ can　　　　　_2_ houses

Reading and Thinking

1. Check the answer that tells what the story is mostly about.
　✓ a long drive
　___ Little Sister's suitcase
　___ Mr. Critter's seat belt

2. Why did Mr. Critter have to keep stopping?
___He had to stop because Little Sister and Little Critter had to use the bathroom.___

3. Little Critter thought they would never get to the ___farm___.

Words such as **he, his, she,** and **her** take the place of other words. Read these sentences. Fill in the blanks.

4. Mr. Critter talked as he drove.
He stands for ___Mr. Critter___.

5. Little Critter packed his bag.
His stands for ___Little Critter's___.

Write **R** by the real things. Write **M** by the make-believe things.

6. _M_ Dogs ride bicycles.

7. _R_ People drive cars.

77

Panel 2 (page 79)

Knowing the Words

Write the words from the story that have these meanings.

1. happy ___glad___
(Par. 1)

2. in between hot and cold ___warm___
(Par. 4)

Check the meaning that fits the underlined word in each sentence.

3. I won't <u>drop</u> the plate.
　___ a little bit of water
　✓ to let go of

4. He put water in the <u>sink</u>.
　✓ part of the kitchen
　___ to go under water

Working with Words

Write **S** beside each word that stands for one of something. Write **P** by each word that stands for more than one.

1. _P_ dishes　　2. _S_ bubble

Circle the right word to finish each sentence. Then write the word in the blank.

3. Little Critter ___knew___ how to help.
(blew (knew) threw)

4. Don't ___splash___ the water!
(crash, flash, (splash))

Reading and Thinking

1. What did Little Critter drop? ___He dropped one plate, one fork, and half a sandwich.___

Write **T** if the sentence is true. Write **F** if it is not true.

2. _T_ This story happens at the farm.

3. _F_ Little Critter does not wash the dishes.

4. What did the Critters have for lunch? ___The Critters had chicken soup, grilled cheese sandwiches, lemonade, and cake.___

5. Why do you think Grandma and Mr. Critter helped out? ___They helped because Little Critter was having some trouble with the bubbles.___

6. How did Little Critter feel when he was helping? ___He felt glad.___

79

Panel 3 (page 81)

Knowing the Words

Write the words from the story that have these meanings.

1. put your arms around
___hugged___
(Par. 1)

2. clothes to wear to bed
___pajamas___
(Par. 5)

Words that mean the same or nearly the same are called **synonyms.** Circle two synonyms in each row.

3. (begin) stop call (start)
4. be (leave) walk (go)
5. listen catch (see) (look)
6. (rush) car (hurry) dog

Learning to Study

Number the words to show A-B-C order for each list.

1. _1_ ask　　2. _4_ set
　 _4_ you　　 _1_ fun
　 _3_ sister　_2_ hug
　 _2_ came　　_3_ mom

Reading and Thinking

1. Check the answer that tells what the story is mostly about.
　___ playing checkers
　___ making a game
　✓ saying goodbye

2. Number the sentences to show what happened first, second, third, and last.
　_3_ Grandpa asked Little Critter to play checkers.
　_1_ Little Critter hugged his parents.
　_2_ Little Critter thought he forgot his pajamas.
　_4_ Little Critter ran into Grandpa.

Write the best word to finish each sentence below.

3. We saw the game and wanted to
___play___
(read, feel, play)

4. Grandpa ___painted___ the checkers.
(painted, tasted, jumped)

81

Panel 4 (page 83)

Knowing the Words

Write the words from the story that have these meanings.

1. something to throw away ___garbage___
(Par. 2)

2. move teeth ___chew___
(Par. 3)

Write **S** for each pair of words that have the same or nearly the same meanings (synonyms). Write **O** for each pair with opposite meanings.

3. little _S_ small

4. easy _O_ hard

5. wash _S_ clean

Circle the three words in each row that belong together.

6. (goat) (cow) (pig) kangaroo
7. (arm) hat (leg) (foot)
8. cup (pants) (shirt) (coat)

Reading and Thinking

1. Number the sentences to show what happened first, second, third, and last.
　_2_ The mother goat chewed Little Critter's pants.
　_1_ Grandpa said that goats can't eat metal.
　_3_ The baby goat chewed Little Critter's shirt.
　_4_ The goats ate out of Little Critter's hand.

2. What was the goat feed made of? ___The goat feed was made of hay, corn, and vegetables.___

3. A baby goat is called a ___kid___ and a mother goat is called a ___nanny___.

Write the best word to finish each sentence below.

4. The goat was ___eating___ Little Critter's shirt.
(eating, chasing, walking)

5. Little Critter ___walked___ past the goat's pen.
(walked, pulled, called)

83

149

Page 85

Write the words from the story that have these meanings.

1. place to sleep ___bed___
_(Par. 1)

2. answered ___replied___
_(Par. 5)

Check the meaning that fits the underlined word in each sentence.

3. Grandma turned off the <u>light</u>.
___ not heavy
_✓_ brightens a room

4. <u>Hand</u> me my teddy bear.
___ part of the body
_✓_ give to

Write a word from the story that stands for each pair of words.

1. can not ___can't___
_(Par. 6)

2. I will ___I'll___
_(Par. 7)

1. Check two sentences that tell how Grandma helped Little Critter.
_✓_ She turned on the night light.
___ She gave him his bicycle.
_✓_ She gave him his teddy bear.

2. How did Little Critter feel when it was time for bed? ___Little Critter was scared.___

3. What did Grandpa do to help Little Critter feel better? ___Grandpa called Little Critter's mom.___

4. Who did Little Critter talk to on the phone? ___Little Critter talked to his mother.___

Write the best word to finish each sentence below.

5. Grandma turned on the ___light___.
(night, light, bright)

6. Little Critter could not ___sleep___.
(sleep, slow, slip)

7. Grandma ___showed___ Little Critter his room.
(turned, called, showed)

85

Page 87

Write the words from the story that have these meanings.

1. noise ___sound___
_(Par. 1)

2. morning meal ___breakfast___
_(Par. 1)

3. animal hair ___fur___
_(Par. 1)

4. a lot ___most___
_(Par. 2)

5. white liquid ___milk___
_(Par. 6)

Circle the three words in each row that belong together.

6. (breakfast) (lunch) food (dinner)
7. (milk) (juice) (water) cereal
8. (bathroom) (kitchen) car (bedroom)
9. (brother) (sister) (father) dog

Walk and **talk** are **rhyming words**. In rhyming words, only the beginning sound is different. Change the **f** in fine to **l, m,** or **n** to make rhyming words. Write each new word.

1. ___line___
2. ___mine___
3. ___nine___

Words such as *he, she,* and *it* take the place of other words. Read these sentences. Then fill in the blanks.

1. Little Critter sang as he worked.
He stands for ___Little Critter___.

2. Little Critter made breakfast and brought it upstairs.
It stands for ___breakfast___.

Write the best word to finish each sentence below.

3. I ___ran___ to be at school on time.
(ran, thought, ate)

4. The children moved the ___toys___ to the backyard.
(street, toys, stairs)

5. The ___clock___ showed we were late.
(flag, chicken, clock)

6. Check the sentence that tells why Grandpa was not in bed.
___ He went to town.
_✓_ He was up early.
___ He was cooking breakfast.

87

Page 89

Check the meaning that fits the underlined word in each sentence.

1. Let's <u>feed</u> the pigs.
_✓_ give food to
___ food for animals

2. <u>Bugs</u> bother pigs.
___ bothers
_✓_ insects

Draw lines to match the words with opposite meanings.

3. enormous — on
4. off — warm
5. cool — tiny

Write a word from the story that can stand for each pair of words.

1. let us ___let's___
_(Par. 1)

2. that is ___that's___
_(Par. 1)

3. they are ___they're___
_(Par. 2)

Make each word mean more than one by adding **-s**. Write the word.

4. piglet ___piglets___

5. bucket ___buckets___

Write **R** by the real things. Write **M** by the make-believe things.

1. _M_ Bugs laugh at pigs.
2. _R_ Pigs roll in the mud.
3. _R_ Pigs have babies.

Write the best word to finish each sentence below.

4. Little Critter ___counted___ twelve piglets.
(counted, wanted, followed)

5. I'll ___wash___ my face and brush my fur.
(light, move, wash)

6. Gabby ___watched___ the man play the game.
(watched, told, filled)

7. We planted ___flowers___ in the garden.
(scraps, puddles, flowers)

89

Page 91

Words that mean the same or nearly the same are called **synonyms**. Use lines to match synonyms.

1. little — quick
2. close — tiny
3. fast — near

A **compound word** is made by putting two words together. Write a compound word for the underlined words below. One is done for you.

A word meaning <u>some</u> kind of <u>thing</u> is *something*.

1. A <u>suit</u> to <u>swim</u> in is a ___swimsuit___.

2. A time <u>after</u> the <u>noon</u> time is ___afternoon___.

Fill in each blank with the right pair of letters to make a word.
ch   sh   th   wh

3. _th_ey   6. _ch_irped
4. lun_ch_   7. fi_sh_
5. _wh_eel   8. su_ch_

1. What was Little Critter afraid of? ___He was afraid of frogs.___

Write **R** by the real things. Write **M** by the make-believe things.

2. _M_ Frogs can fly.
3. _R_ Crickets chirp.
4. _M_ Fish wear swimsuits.
5. _R_ Butterflies fly.

6. Check the answer that tells what time of year it is in the story.
___ fall
_✓_ summer
___ winter

91

150

Page 93

Write the words from the story that have these meanings.

1. afternoon meal
   __lunch__
   (Par. 1)

2. keeps food cold
   __refrigerator__
   (Par. 4)

3. well known
   __famous__
   (Par. 8)

Circle the three words in each row that belong together.

4. (pickles) (orange juice) plates (bread)
5. (front) candy (side) (back)
6. milk (plates) (dishes) (bowls)

A **compound word** is made by putting two words together. Use these words to make two compound words.

   tast   box   bread   break

1. __breadbox__   2. __breakfast__

1. Check the answer that tells what the story is mostly about.
   ____ how to make a sandwich
   ____ what Little Critter makes for breakfast
   _✓_ what Little Critter makes for lunch

2. Write two things that Little Critter used to make the sandwiches.
   __Answers may include: peanut__
   __butter, pickles, orange juice,__
   __or potato chips.__

3. Write T if the sentence is true. Write F if it is not true.
   _F_ The story takes place at night.
   _T_ Little Critter made his favorite lunch.
   _F_ Little Critter was sad.

Write the best word to finish each sentence below.

4. The house was __quiet__ after the party ended.
   (quiet, scared, angry)

5. My sister and her __friends__ took a trip.
   (field, friends, fence)

93

Page 95

Write the words from the story that have these meanings.

1. baby cow __calf__
   (Par. 3)

2. not rough __smooth__
   (Par. 5)

3. why __because__
   (Par. 6)

4. a lot __much__
   (Par. 7)

In each row, circle the two words with opposite meanings.

5. (down) off around (up)
6. tell (went) say (came)
7. show (large) (small) grass

Circle the right word to finish each sentence. Then write the word in the blank.

1. My mother opened a __can__ of soup for lunch.
   (can) cane)

2. Will you __hide__ the gift for the party?
   (hid (hide))

3. Does your new hat __fit__?
   (fit) fight)

1. Check the answer that tells what the story is mostly about.
   _✓_ milking the cows
   ____ ice cream
   ____ milking machines

Write T if the sentence is true. Write F if it is not true.

2. _T_ Grandma and Grandpa could milk all their cows.
3. _F_ Little Critter was afraid to feed Jody.

4. Check the sentence that tells how cows and people are like each other.
   ____ They both have four legs.
   ____ They both have four stomachs.
   _✓_ They both have babies.

Write R by the real things. Write M by the make-believe things.

5. _R_ Some farms use milking machines.
6. _M_ Cows have five stomachs.
7. _R_ Cheese can be made from milk.

95

Page 97

Write the words from the story that have these meanings.

1. in back of
   __behind__
   (Par. 6)

2. what something tastes like
   __flavor__
   (Par. 8)

Check the meaning that fits the underlined word in each sentence.

3. Little Critter went to the blackberry patch.
   ____ to fix a hole in something
   _✓_ a small area

4. Little Critter picked blackberries.
   ____ gather from trees
   _✓_ collected

Write a word from the story that can stand for each pair of words.

1. We are __We're__
   (Par. 4)

2. cannot __can't__
   (Par. 10)

An **'s** shows that a thing belongs to someone. Change these words to show what belongs to someone.

3. Grandma_'s_ bowl
4. Grandpa_'s_ berries

1. Who picked more berries?
   __Grandma picked more__
   __berries.__

2. What kind of berries did Little Critter and Grandma pick?
   __They picked blackberries.__

3. Why wasn't Little Critter's bowl full?
   __Little Critter ate his berries.__

Write T if the sentence is true. Write F if it is not true.

4. _T_ Grandma wanted to make pies.
5. _F_ Little Critter did not eat any berries.
6. _F_ Little Critter does not like berries.

97

Page 99

Write the words from the story that have these meanings.

1. put two different things together
   __mixed__
   (Par. 1)

2. tastes very good __delicious__
   (Par. 4)

3. Check the meaning that fits the underlined word in the sentence.

   Little Critter put hearts on top of the pie.
   ____ a toy that spins
   _✓_ highest part

To put words in A-B-C order you must first look at the first letter of each word. If the first letters are the same, look at the second letters. Number each list to show A-B-C order.

1. _3_ flour   2. _1_ pie
   _1_ berries   _2_ plate
   _2_ crust   _3_ pour
   _4_ oven   _4_ put

1. Check the answer that tells what the story is mostly about.
   _✓_ baking blackberry pies
   ____ turning on the oven
   ____ washing blackberries

2. Number the sentences to show what happened first, second, third, and last.
   _4_ They put the last pie in the oven.
   _3_ Little Critter decorated the top of the pie.
   _2_ Grandma got the flour out of the cupboard.
   _1_ Grandma and Little Critter washed the berries.

Write T if the sentence is true. Write F if it is not true.

3. _T_ Pie crust is made of flour and shortening.
   _F_ Pies do not need to be baked.

4. What did Grandma teach Little Critter about making a pie?
   __Answers may include: how to__
   __make dough, how to make__
   __crust, how to decorate the__
   __top of the pie, how to fill the__
   __pie, how to bake the pie.__

99

Page 101

Knowing the Words

Write the words from the story that have these meanings.

1. place where things grow __garden__
(Par. 1)

2. ready to eat __ripe__
(Par. 5)

Circle the three words in each row that belong together.

3. (nap) (dream) sight (sleep)
4. (beets) (potatoes) (carrots) flowers
5. sky (trees) (flowers) (plants)

Working with Words

Write the best word to finish each sentence below.

1. Do you __know__ the new teacher?
(know, nose, noise)

2. Did someone __knock__ on the door?
(nest, lock, knock)

Write these compound words beside their meanings.

underground   blackberry
afternoon

3. a berry that is black __blackberry__
4. later than noon __afternoon__
5. under the ground __underground__

Reading and Thinking

1. What color are tomatoes that are not ready to eat? __They are green.__

2. Check two sentences that show that potatoes grow underground.
___ Potatoes taste good.
✓ Little Critter did not see any potatoes above the ground.
✓ Little Critter dug up the potatoes.

3. How are carrots like potatoes? __They grow underground.__

Write R by the real things. Write M by the make-believe things.

4. __M__ Potatoes can walk.
__R__ Vegetables grow in the garden.
__M__ Little Critter is a pumpkin.

101

Page 103

Knowing the Words

Write the words from the story that have these meanings.

1. being polite __manners__
(Par. 2)

2. pain __ache__
(Par. 6)

3. not sweet __sour__
(Par. 9)

Circle the three words in each row that belong together.

4. (taste) (eat) (chew) move
5. (wonderful) sour (delicious) (good)

Working with Words

In each sentence, circle three words with the same vowel sound as the word in dark print.

1. now   The (cow) (found) the sweet grass and gave a (loud) MOO!

2. now   (How) can I drive (around) the (mountain)?

Reading and Thinking

1. Check the answer that tells what the story is mostly about.
___ Little Critter doesn't like vegetables.
✓ Little Critter tries a new vegetable.
___ Grandpa bought new hens in town.

2. What did Little Critter think beets would taste like? Why? __He thought beets would taste sweet. He thought they would taste like the blackberries because they are purple.__

3. How do you know that Grandma likes beets? __Grandma said they were delicious.__

Write T if the sentence is true. Write F if it is not true.

4. __F__ Little Critter likes beets.
__T__ Grandma likes beets.
__T__ Grandpa gave Little Critter some candy.

5. Check two answers that describe Little Critter.
___ He is mean.
✓ He helps out.
✓ He has good manners.

103

Page 105

Knowing the Words

In each row, circle two words that have opposite meanings.

1. see (close) (far) look
2. (never) few (always) some
3. cry break (sleep) (wake)

Working with Words

A word part that can be said by itself is called a **syllable**. Some words have two consonants between two vowels. These words can be divided between the consonants, as in pic|nic. In each word below, draw a line to divide the word into syllables.

1. s u m|m e r   3. c o t|t o n
2. s u d|d e n   4. c o n|t e s t

Walk and **talk** are **rhyming words**. In rhyming words, only the beginning sound is different. Write words that rhyme with **spray** by changing **spr** in **spray** to **p** or **w**.

5. __pay__   6. __way__

Then use each new word in the right sentence.

7. Grandpa will show you the __way__ to the fair.
8. We must __pay__ for our tickets.

Reading and Thinking

1. Check the answer that tells what the story is mostly about.
___ the pie contest
___ cotton candy
✓ the fair

Write the best word to finish each sentence below.

2. I want to play that __game__ with Grandpa. (warm, game, tent)

3. Little Critter looked all __around__ the fair. (around, above, behind)

4. The clown had a bright red __mouth__
(jelly, garden, mouth)

Read these sentences. Then fill in the blanks.

5. Grandpa sneezed as he played the game.
He stands for __Grandpa__.

6. Grandma heard music as she walked by the tent.
She stands for __Grandma__.

7. The ice cream melted as it sat on the table.
It stands for __the ice cream__.

105

Page 107

Knowing the Words

Words that mean the same or nearly the same are called **synonyms**. Circle two synonyms in each row.

1. (scream) ride spin (yell)
2. worker (belt) (strap) stay
3. (glad) sad wobble (happy)

Working with Words

Words that end in s, ss, x, sh, or ch add **-es** to show more than one. Rewrite these words to show more than one. One is done for you.

dress   _dresses_
1. box   __boxes__
2. kiss   __kisses__
3. watch   __watches__

Circle the right word to finish each sentence. Then write the word in the blank.

4. He __rode__ his bicycle around the farm. (rod (rode))

5. Little Critter wanted some __ice__ in his soda pop. (is (ice))

6. That __ride__ makes me dizzy. (ride) rid)

Reading and Thinking

1. Number the sentences to show what happened first, second, third, and last.
__4__ Grandpa asked Little Critter if he was okay.
__1__ Little Critter did not want to ride the merry-go-round.
__2__ The fair worker fastened Little Critter's safety belt.
__3__ Little Critter was happy when the ride was over.

2. Why did Little Critter feel dizzy? __He felt dizzy because the ride spun around.__

Write T if the sentence is true. Write F if it is not true.

3. __F__ The ride was called the Tiny Teacup.
4. __T__ Grandpa did not go on the ride.
5. __F__ Little Critter was the only one on the ride.

6. Why didn't Little Critter want to go on the merry-go-round at first? __He said the merry-go-round was for littler critters.__

7. What changed his mind? __The teacup ride made him too dizzy.__

107

152

Top Left Panel (page 109)

Check the meaning that fits the underlined word in each sentence.

1. Can I go <u>watch</u> the pie-eating contest?
   _____ small clock
   ✓ look at

2. I will <u>save</u> you a piece of pie.
   ✓ set aside
   _____ rescue

3. Did she <u>run</u> in the race?
   ✓ move fast on legs
   _____ what a machine does

Learning to Study

To put words in A-B-C order you must first look at the first letter of each word. If the first letters are the same, look at the second letters. Number each list to show A-B-C order.

1. 3 sign   3. 3 tent
   4 stomach   2 tasting
   1 saved   1 begin
   2 set   4 their

2. 4 pie   4. 3 red
   2 faces   1 fur
   1 contest   4 ribbon
   3 judges   2 read

Use the groups of words in the box to finish the sentences below.

> • she thought he would like to eat it
> • he was hungry
> • he smelled pie

1. Little Critter ate the cherry pie because _he was hungry_ .

2. Little Critter's stomach growled louder when _he smelled pie_ .

3. Grandma saved a piece of pie for Little Critter because _she thought he would like to eat it_ .

109

Top Right Panel (page 111)

Write the words from the story that have these meanings.

1. place to deliver letters _mailbox_
   (Par. 1)

2. like the most _favorites_
   (Par. 2)

3. day before today _yesterday_
   (Par. 3)

In each row, circle the two words with opposite meanings.

4. (close) tiny (far) little
5. (hot) (cold) tiny ice
6. smooth (hardest) (softest) loudest

Working with Words

The ending -er means "more," so **prouder** means "more proud." The ending -est means "most," so **proudest** means "most proud." Add the endings -er and -est to these base words. One is done for you.

Malcolm is the tall_est_ of six boys.

1. Little Critter is old_er_ than Little Sister.
2. I was the loud_est_ of the four.

1. Write two things that Little Critter's mom and dad wrote about in their letter.
   Answers may include: they went to the zoo, the weather was warm, or they got ice cream, etc.

Write **T** if the sentence is true. Write **F** if it is not true.

2. _T_ Little Critter is having fun at the farm.
3. _F_ Little Sister is at the farm.
4. _T_ Little Critter's family misses him.
5. _F_ Little Critter does not help Grandma and Grandpa.
6. _T_ Grandma and Grandpa are glad to have Little Critter visit.

7. Mom, Dad, and Little Sister went to the _zoo_ and got some _ice cream_ afterwards.

Write the best word to finish each sentence.

8. Grandma _found_ a letter in the mailbox. (found, hid, woke)
9. The girl _waved_ her hand to show she was ready. (washed, bit, waved)

111

Bottom Left Panel (page 113)

Write the words from the story that have these meanings.

1. shut _closed_
   (Par. 1)

2. hard rain _storm_
   (Par. 2)

3. scared _afraid_
   (Par. 8)

Check the meaning that fits the underlined word in each sentence.

4. You are <u>safe</u> inside.
   _____ place to keep money
   ✓ won't be hurt

5. I'm glad the storm is <u>over</u>.
   _____ on the other side
   ✓ done, finished

6. My <u>ears</u> hurt from the noise.
   _____ parts of corn plants
   ✓ things used for hearing

Learning to Study

Number the words to show A-B-C order for each list.

1. 4 thunder   2. 2 need
   2 here   3 night
   1 hard   1 eyes
   3 storm   4 now

1. Number the sentences to show what happened first, second, third, and last.
   2 Little Critter dove under the bed.
   1 There was a loud crash of thunder.
   4 Little Critter wasn't scared anymore.
   3 Grandpa told Little Critter a story.

2. Check two answers that show Little Critter was scared.
   ✓ Little Critter squeezed Grandpa's hand.
   _____ Little Critter went to sleep.
   ✓ Little Critter dove under the bed.

Write **R** by the real things. Write **M** by the make-believe things.

3. _R_ Thunder is a loud noise.
4. _M_ A storm can laugh.

Write the best word to finish each sentence below.
5. Thunder can be very _loud_. (loud, flat, bright)
6. Lightning can be very _bright_. (loud, bright, furry)

113

Bottom Right Panel (page 115)

Write the words from the story that have these meanings.

1. keep safe _protect_
   (Par. 5)

2. seat put on a horse _saddle_
   (Par. 6)

Working with Words

Write the best word to finish each sentence below.

1. Storms can bring _rain_. (rain, ran, run)
2. Can you _say_ the new word? (said, sad, say)
3. I _know_ the answer. (now, know, not)

An **'s** at the end of a word shows that a thing belongs to someone or something. Change these groups of words by using **'s**.

4. the saddle of the horse
   the _horse's_ saddle

5. the farm of Grandpa
   Grandpa's farm

1. What did Grandpa say did not hurt the horses?
   He said the horseshoes did not hurt the horses.

2. Check the answer that tells what the story is mostly about.
   _____ how to put shoes on horses
   ✓ taking care of horses
   _____ Old Kicker

3. Check two sentences that tell why Little Critter may not want to ride Old Kicker.
   ✓ Old Kicker whinnied loudly.
   _____ Old Kicker had a saddle on.
   ✓ Old Kicker jumped up on his hind legs.

4. List two things that can be done to care for horses.
   Answers may include: feeding them, cleaning their stalls, brushing their coats, or riding them.

115

Page 117

Reading and Thinking

1. Check the answer that tells what the story is mostly about.
   - _____ making wool blankets
   - _____ cleaning the sheep pen
   - ✓ learning about sheep

Read these sentences. Then fill in the blanks.

2. Grandma talked while she sheared the sheep.
   She stands for _____Grandma_____

3. The lamb pulled the bottle as it drank.
   It stands for _____the lamb_____

4. Little Critter laughed as he chased the lamb.
   He stands for _____Little Critter_____

Working with Words

Write the best word to finish each sentence below.

1. I have a __pin__ on my dress.
   (pen, pine, pin)
2. Can you __ride__ the horse?
   (ride, red, roll)
3. That book is __mine__.
   (win, mine, men)
4. Will you feed the __cat__?
   (can, car, cat)
5. The boys __cook__ their lunch.
   (cook, look, book)

When **re-** is added to a word, it changes the meaning of the word. The word part **re-** means "again." **Refill** means "fill again." Add **re-** to these words to finish the sentences.

6. I will __re__build the house.
7. Who will __re__do these papers?
8. Please __re__fill the tall jar.
9. Did you __re__write the test?
10. Did the station __re__run the show?
11. Please __re__tell the story.

117

Page 119

Working with Words

Write a compound word for the underlined words in each sentence.

1. A <u>yard</u> that is part of a <u>farm</u> is a _____farmyard_____
2. A <u>storm</u> that brings <u>snow</u> is a _____snowstorm_____

Write the best word to finish each sentence below.

3. Be sure to look over __each__ answer. (each ears)
4. Little Critter saw a __turtle__ (turkey turtle)
5. Little Critter rode his __bicycle__ (tricycle bicycle)
6. __Try__ to do your best. (Try Fry)

Reading and Thinking

1. Number the sentences to show what happened first, second, third, and last.
   - _1_ Little Critter wanted to go on a bike ride.
   - _3_ Little Critter saw a turtle.
   - _2_ Grandpa had to finish some chores.
   - _4_ Little Critter wanted to tell Little Sister about the turtle.

Write the best word to finish each sentence.

2. The child took the __little__ puppy for a walk. (deep, little, helmet)
3. Can you see your __face__ in the glass? (family, idea, face)

Look at the picture with the story. Write the best word to finish each sentence about the picture.

4. Little Critter has a __red__ helmet. (red, blue, yellow)
5. There are __trees__ along the paths. (trees, roads, cars)
6. The farmyard is __clean__ (dirty, clean, moving)

119

Page 121

Knowing the Words

In each row, circle the two words with opposite meanings.

1. cool   cold   (big)   (little)
2. (light)   old   used   (heavy)

Working with Words

Walk and **talk** are rhyming words. In rhyming words, only the beginning sound is different. The missing words below rhyme with **shook**. Change **sh** in **shook** to **l, b, c,** and **t.** Then write each new word in the right sentence.

1. __look__   3. __cook__
2. __book__   4. __took__

5. We __took__ the wrong road.
6. Did you read the __book__?
7. I can __cook__ dinner.
8. Did the car __look__ new?

Write the best word to finish each sentence below.

9. I have not __seen__ her before. (send seen)
10. We rode the __bus__ to school. (bone bus)

Reading and Thinking

1. Check the answer that tells what the story is mostly about.
   - _____ a picture of Little Sister
   - _____ Grandma's sandwiches
   - ✓ a letter from Little Sister

Read these sentences. Then fill in the blanks.

2. Grandma cooked as she talked to Little Critter.
   She stands for _____Grandma_____

3. Little Critter held the letter as he read it to Grandma.
   It stands for _____the letter_____

Write the best word to finish each sentence below.

4. The friends __write__ letters at camp. (tell, write, do)
5. Some animals __eat__ berries. (make, buy, eat)
6. Did you __drink__ the milk? (stay, drink, grow)
7. Why do you think Little Sister was playing with Little Critter's toys?
   _____Answers will vary._____

121

Page 123

Knowing the Words

Circle the three words in each row that belong together.

1. (apples)   (oranges)   cats   (bananas)
2. (chicken)   dog   (turkey)   (peacock)
3. (cookie)   (cake)   (candy)   pizza
4. cake   (water)   (milk)   (juice)

Working with Words

Write the best word to finish each sentence below.

1. The class will __care__ for the bird. (care car)
2. Did someone __burn__ dinner? (barn burn)

Most words add **-s** or **-es** to show more than one. Words that end in **y** are different. In most words that end in **y**, change the **y** to **i**, and add **-es**. Change the words below to mean more than one. One is done for you.

berry — _berries_
3. story — _stories_
4. penny — _pennies_
5. puppy — _puppies_
6. library — _libraries_

Reading and Thinking

1. Check the answer that tells what the story is mostly about.
   - ✓ a picnic
   - _____ eating apples
   - _____ peanut butter and pickle sandwiches

2. Why couldn't Little Critter eat the apples?
   He couldn't eat the apples because they wouldn't be ready until fall.

3. Why is Grandma's picnic a "balanced" meal?
   Grandma's meal had all the different food groups.

4. What would you pack for a healthy picnic?
   Answers will vary.
   _____

5. Check three answers that are healthy snacks.
   - _____ potato chips
   - ✓ strawberries
   - ✓ carrot sticks
   - _____ candy
   - ✓ raisins

123

Page 125

Write the words from the story that have these meanings.

1. black birds ___crows___ (Par. 2)

2. not after ___before___ (Par. 2)

Circle the right word to finish the sentence. Then write the word in the blank.

1. I finished ___first___ grade.
   (**first**) forest)

2. You are too ___short___ to reach the top. (sharp (**short**))

The letter **c** can stand for the sound of **s** as in **city** and **k** as in **cat**. Circle words that have **c** as in **city**. Cross out words that have a **c** as in **cat**.

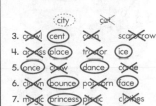

(city)   ~~cat~~

3. ~~crawl~~ (cent) ~~corn~~ scare~~crow~~
4. a~~cross~~ (place) tra~~ctor~~ (ice)
5. (once) ~~claw~~ (dance) ~~come~~
6. ~~clown~~ (bounce) pop~~corn~~ (face)
7. ma~~gic~~ (princess) pla~~stic~~ ~~clothes~~

1. Number the sentences to show what happened first, second, third, and last.

   __3__ Grandpa and Little Critter made a scarecrow.

   __1__ The crows were eating the corn.

   __4__ Little Critter said, "Watch out crows!"

   __2__ Grandpa gathered some hay.

2. What did Grandpa and Little Critter make the scarecrow out of?
   They made the scarecrow out of hay, old clothes, rope, and a rag.

3. Why did Grandpa want to make a scarecrow? He wanted to scare the crows away.

4. The crows are scared of a scarecrow because it looks like a real person.

5. Do you think the scarecrow will work? Why? Answers will vary.

125

Page 127

Write the words from the story that have these meanings.

1. pointy ___sharp___ (Par. 3)

2. center ___middle___ (Par. 3)

3. wet ___soggy___ (Par. 5)

A word part that can be said by itself is called a **syllable**. Some words have two consonants between two vowels. These words can be divided between the consonants, as in **pic|nic**. Write each word below. Then draw a line to divide the word into syllables.

1. little ___lit|tle___
2. soggy ___sog|gy___
3. middle ___mid|dle___

Circle the right word to finish each sentence. Then write the word in the blank.

4. Did you hear the ___knock___?
   (knew, (knock) know)

5. I knew that was the ___wrong___ answer. (write, (wrong) wrote)

1. Number the sentences to show what happened first, second, third, and last.

   __1__ All the chores were done.

   __3__ Little Critter cast his line into the pond.

   __2__ Grandpa and Little Critter went to the pond.

   __4__ Grandpa's hat got wet.

2. What did Grandpa show Little Critter how to do?
   Grandpa showed Little Critter how to put the worm on the fishhook.

3. Check two sentences that tell about the pond.
   ___ Sharks live there.
   _✓_ Frogs live there.
   _✓_ Fish live there.
   ___ There is no water.

127

Page 129

1. Check the answer that tells what the story is mostly about.
   ___ buying a kite
   _✓_ buying some marbles
   ___ saving money

Write the best word to finish each sentence.

2. Please ___think___ before you answer. (carry, hide, think)

3. We ran ___toward___ the house in the rain. (toward, over, away)

Look at the picture on this page. Answer these questions about it.

4. What else does the general store sell?
   Answers may include: marbles, cards, or yo-yos.

5. What is Little Critter doing?
   He is playing with a yo-yo.

The ending -y added to a word can mean "full of." The word **rainy** means "full of rain." Write the meanings for these words. One is done for you.

dirty ___full of dirt___

1. grassy ___full of grass___
2. creamy ___full of cream___

In rhyming words, only the beginning sound is different. In each sentence, write the word from the box that rhymes with the underlined word.

soap	bright	caught

3. Late at night, the stars are very ___bright___

4. I hope that I can find the ___soap___

5. My mother bought the fish that I ___caught___

Circle the right word to finish each sentence. Write the word in the blank.

6. We played, ___but___ we lost. (bit, bat, (but))

7. Did you find your ___hat___? (hit, (hat) hot)

129

Page 131

1. Check the answer that tells what the story is mostly about.
   ___ crayons and paper
   _✓_ a present for Grandma and Grandpa
   ___ Grandpa's nap

2. Why did Little Critter go upstairs?
   He went upstairs because Grandma and Grandpa were busy.

3. What did Little Critter give to Grandma and Grandpa?
   He gave them a card and two marbles.

4. Why do you think Grandma said the marbles were a treasure?
   Answers will vary.

Fill in each blank with the right pair of letters to make a word.

ar   er   or

1. Will you read me a st_or_y?

2. We worked with flashc_ar_ds.

3. She took h_er_ book home.

The letter **g** can stand for the sound of **j** as in **cage** and **g** as in **girl**. Circle words that have **g** as in **cage**. Cross out words that have **g** as in **girl**.

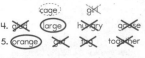

(cage)   ~~girl~~

4. ~~dog~~ (large) hu~~ngry~~ ~~goose~~
5. (orange) ~~dog~~ ~~big~~ to~~gether~~

Write the compound words that can be made from the words below.

sun   thing   shine   any

6. ___sunshine___   7. ___anything___

In each sentence, circle two words with the same vowel sound as the word in dark print.

8. **soap**   Wear your (coat) when you walk down the (road.)

9. **grow**   I can (throw) the ball (low.)

131

155

Top Left Panel (page 133)

Reading and Thinking

1. Grandma made some funny ___pancakes___ for Little Critter.

2. What didn't Little Critter like?
   __He didn't like coffee.__

Write **T** if the sentence is true. Write **F** if it is not true.

3. __F__ Little Critter likes coffee.
4. __T__ Grandpa drinks coffee.
5. __F__ Grandpa was eating eggs for breakfast.

6. Do you think Little Critter liked the pancakes? Why?
   __Answers will vary.__

Working with Words

Circle words that have **c** as in **city**. Cross out words that have **c** as in **cat**.

1. ~~picture~~   ~~uncle~~   (bounce)   (nice)
2. ~~pancake~~   ~~corner~~   (face)   ~~ice~~
3. (fence)   ~~across~~   ~~candy~~   (dance)

An **'s** at the end of a word may be used to show that something belongs to someone. Change these groups of words using **'s**.

4. the pancake of Little Critter
   __Little Critter's__ pancake

5. the coffee that belongs to Grandpa
   __Grandpa's__ coffee

6. the breakfast of Grandma
   __Grandma's__ breakfast

Circle the right word to finish each sentence. Then write the word in the blank.

7. I can't __think__ of it.
   (think) thank, tent)

8. She __bit__ into the apple.
   (bat, (bit) but)

133

Top Right Panel (page 135)

Knowing the Words

Write the words from the story that have these meanings.

1. a game __checkers__
   (Par. 3)

2. made a sad face __frowned__
   (Par. 4)

Working with Words

Circle the right word. Write it in the blank.

1. Hold on to the __string__ of the kite. (string) spring)

2. We planted a __tree__ in the yard. (tree) free)

3. Say the word **bake**. Listen to the vowel sound of the word. In each word below, circle the two letters that stand for that sound.
   afr(ai)d   st(ay)   aw(ay)   p(ai)nt

The letter **g** can stand for the sound of **j** as in **cage** and **g** as in **girl**. Circle words that have **g** as in **girl**. Cross out words that have **g** as in **cage**.

(girl)   ~~cage~~

4. ~~general~~   ~~village~~   (big)   (bag)
5. ~~danger~~   (goats)   ~~large~~   (again)
6. (dog)   ~~strange~~   ~~orange~~   (game)

Reading and Thinking

1. Why did Little Critter play checkers with Little Sister?
   __He wanted to cheer her up.__

Write **T** if the sentence is true. Write **F** if it is not true.

2. __F__ Little Critter was angry.
3. __T__ Little Sister had fun playing checkers.

4. How did Little Sister feel after Little Critter played with her?
   __Little Sister was happy after__
   __Little Critter played with her.__

135

Bottom Left Panel (page 137)

Knowing the Words

Write the words from the story that have these meanings.

1. to go see someone
   __visit__
   (Par. 4)

2. did not forget
   __remembered__
   (Par. 6)

Working with Words

Use these words to make compound words. Then use the compound words to finish each sentence below.

every   farm   thing   yard

1. Thank you for __everything__
2. The sheep live in the __farmyard__

An **'s** at the end of a word may be used to show that something belongs to someone. Change these groups of words using **'s**.

3. the animals of Grandpa
   __Grandpa's animals__

4. the barn of the horse
   __the horse's barn__

5. the hat of mom
   __mom's hat__

Reading and Thinking

1. Check the answer that tells what the story is mostly about.
   ___ following Little Critter
   ✓ saying good-bye
   ___ talking to animals

2. What was Little Sister doing in the story? __Little Sister was__
   __following Little Critter.__

3. Check the sentence that tells why Little Critter looked sad.
   ✓ He was going to miss the farm.
   ___ He didn't like the animals.
   ___ Little Sister made him cry.

4. Who will take care of the animals when Grandma and Grandpa come for a visit? __their friends__

5. Check the sentence that tells why Little Critter won't be sad.
   ___ He is going to live at the farm.
   ___ Little Sister gave him some money.
   ✓ Grandma and Grandpa are coming for a visit soon.

6. How did Little Critter show his good manners? __He said thank you__
   __to Grandma and Grandpa.__

137

Bottom Right Panel (page 139)

Reading and Thinking

1. Number the sentences to show what happened first, second, third, and last.
   __2__ Little Critter's mom and dad said good night.
   __4__ Little Critter went back to sleep.
   __1__ Little Critter was glad to see his own room.
   __3__ Little Critter remembered he was at home.

2. Where did Little Critter think he was when he woke up?
   __He thought he was still at__
   __the farm.__

Working with Words

Rewrite these words to mean more than one. Remember to change the **y** to **i** before adding **-es**.

1. country __countries__
2. city __cities__
3. family __families__

4. Say the word **keep**. Listen to the vowel sound in the word. In each word below, circle the two letters that stand for that sound.

   f(ee)t   (ea)ch   s(ee)d   d(ee)p

The spelling of some base words is changed before an ending is added. Words such as **happy** must have the **y** changed to **i** before adding an ending. Endings are word parts like **-er**, **-est**, and **-ed**. Change the **y** to **i** and add the endings to these words. One is done for you.

carry + ed   _carried_
5. heavy + est   __heaviest__
6. hurry + ed   __hurried__
7. merry + er   __merrier__
8. hungry + est   __hungriest__

139

SPECTRUM

SPECTRUM WORKBOOKS
ILLUSTRATED BY MERCER MAYER!

Grades K–2 • 128–160 full-color pages • Size: 8.375" x 10.875" • Paperback

McGraw-Hill, the premier educational publisher for grades PreK–12, and acclaimed children's author and illustrator, Mercer Mayer, are the proud creators of this workbook line featuring the lovable Little Critter. Like other Spectrum titles, the length, breadth, and depth of the activities in these workbooks enable children to learn a variety of skills about a single subject.

• Mercer Mayer's Little Critter family of characters has sold over 50 million books. These wholesome characters and stories appeal to both parents and teachers.

• Each full-color workbook is based on highly respected McGraw-Hill Companies' textbooks.

• All exercises feature easy-to-follow instructions.

• An answer key is included in each workbook.

TITLE	ISBN	PRICE
LANGUAGE ARTS		
Gr. K	1-57768-840-6	$7.95
Gr. 1	1-57768-841-4	$7.95
Gr. 2	1-57768-842-2	$7.95
MATH		
Gr. K	1-57768-800-7	$7.95
Gr. 1	1-57768-801-5	$7.95
Gr. 2	1-57768-802-3	$7.95
PHONICS		
Gr. K	1-57768-820-1	$7.95
Gr. 1	1-57768-821-X	$7.95
Gr. 2	1-57768-822-8	$7.95
READING		
Gr. K	1-57768-810-4	$7.95
Gr. 1	1-57768-811-2	$7.95
Gr. 2	1-57768-812-0	$7.95
SPELLING		
Gr. K	1-57768-830-9	$7.95
Gr. 1	1-57768-831-7	$7.95
Gr. 2	1-57768-832-5	$7.95
WRITING		
Gr. K	1-57768-850-3	$7.95
Gr. 1	1-57768-851-1	$7.95
Gr. 2	1-57768-852-X	$7.95

Prices subject to change without notice.

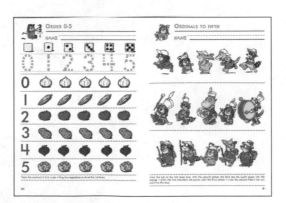

Wholesome, well-known characters
plus proven school curriculum
equals learning success!

SPECTRUM

Brought to you by McGraw-Hill, the premier educational publisher for grades PreK–12.
All our workbooks meet school curriculum guidelines and correspond to
The McGraw-Hill Companies' classroom textbooks.

LANGUAGE ARTS

Grades 2–6 • 160 full-color pages
Size: 8.375" x 10.875" • Paperback

Encourages creativity and builds confidence by making writing fun! Sixty four-part lessons strengthen writing skills by focusing on parts of speech, word usage, sentence structure, punctuation, and proofreading. This series is based on the highly respected SRA/McGraw-Hill language arts series. Answer key included.

MATH

Grades K–8 • Over 150 pages
Size: 8.375" x 10.875" • Paperback

Features easy-to-follow instructions that give students a clear path to success. This series includes comprehensive coverage of the basic skills, helping children master math fundamentals. Answer key included.

PHONICS/WORD STUDY

Grades K–6 • Over 200 pages
Size: 8.375" x 10.875" • Paperback

Provides everything children need to build multiple skills in language arts. This series focuses on phonics, structural analysis, and dictionary skills, and offers creative ideas for using phonics and word study skills in language areas. Answer key included.

TITLE	ISBN	PRICE
LANGUAGE ARTS		
Gr. 3	1-57768-483-4	$7.95
Gr. 4	1-57768-484-2	$7.95
Gr. 5	1-57768-485-0	$7.95
Gr. 6	1-57768-486-9	$7.95
MATH		
Gr. K	1-57768-400-1	$7.95
Gr. 1	1-57768-401-X	$7.95
Gr. 2	1-57768-402-8	$7.95
Gr. 3	1-57768-403-6	$7.95
Gr. 4	1-57768-404-4	$7.95
Gr. 5	1-57768-405-2	$7.95
Gr. 6	1-57768-406-0	$7.95
Gr. 7	1-57768-407-9	$7.95
Gr. 8	1-57768-408-7	$7.95
PHONICS (Grades K–3)/WORD STUDY and PHONICS (Grades 4–6)		
Gr. K	1-57768-450-8	$7.95
Gr. 1	1-57768-451-6	$7.95
Gr. 2	1-57768-452-4	$7.95
Gr. 3	1-57768-453-2	$7.95
Gr. 4	1-57768-454-0	$7.95
Gr. 5	1-57768-455-9	$7.95
Gr. 6	1-57768-456-7	$7.95

Prices subject to change without notice.

SPECTRUM offers comprehensive coverage of basic skills.

READING

Grades K–6 • Over 150 full-color pages
Size: 8.375" x 10.875" • Paperback

This full-color series creates an enjoyable reading environment, even for below-average readers. Each book contains captivating content, colorful characters, and compelling illustrations, so children are eager to find out what happens next. Answer key included.

SPELLING

Grades 3–6 • 160 full-color pages
Size: 8.375" x 10.875" • Paperback

This full-color series links spelling to reading and writing, and increases skills in words and meanings, consonant and vowel spellings, and proofreading practice. Speller dictionary and answer key included.

TEST PREP

Grades 1–8 • 160 full-color pages
Size: 8.375" x 10.875" • Paperback

This series teaches the skills, strategies, and techniques necessary for students to succeed on any standardized test. Each book contains guidelines and advice for parents along with study tips for students. Grades 1 and 2 cover Reading, Language Arts, Writing, and Math. Grades 3 through 8 cover Reading, Language Arts, Writing, Math, Social Studies, and Science.

WRITING

Grades 3–6 • 160 full-color pages
Size: 8.375" x 10.875" • Paperback

Lessons focus on creative and expository writing using clearly stated objectives and pre-writing exercises. Eight essential reading skills are applied. Activities include main idea, sequence, comparison, detail, fact and opinion, cause and effect, making a point, and point of view. Each level includes a Writer's Handbook that offers writing tips. Answer key included.

FLASH CARDS

Card size: 3.0625" x 4.5625"

Flash cards provide children with one of the most effective ways to drill and practice fundamentals. The cards have large type, making it easy for young learners to read them. Each pack contains 50 flash cards including a parent instruction card that offers suggestions for fun, creative activities and games that reinforce children's skills development.

TITLE	ISBN	PRICE
READING		
Gr. K	1-57768-460-5	$7.95
Gr. 1	1-57768-461-3	$7.95
Gr. 2	1-57768-462-1	$7.95
Gr. 3	1-57768-463-X	$7.95
Gr. 4	1-57768-464-8	$7.95
Gr. 5	1-57768-465-6	$7.95
Gr. 6	1-57768-466-4	$7.95
SPELLING		
Gr. 3	1-57768-493-1	$7.95
Gr. 4	1-57768-494-X	$7.95
Gr. 5	1-57768-495-8	$7.95
Gr. 6	1-57768-496-6	$7.95
TEST PREP		
Gr. 1–2	1-57768-662-4	$9.95
Gr. 3	1-57768-663-2	$9.95
Gr. 4	1-57768-664-0	$9.95
Gr. 5	1-57768-665-9	$9.95
Gr. 6	1-57768-666-7	$9.95
Gr. 7	1-57768-667-5	$9.95
Gr. 8	1-57768-668-3	$9.95
WRITING		
Gr. 3	1-57768-913-5	$7.95
Gr. 4	1-57768-914-3	$7.95
Gr. 5	1-57768-915-1	$7.95
Gr. 6	1-57768-916-X	$7.95
FLASH CARDS		
Addition	1-57768-167-3	$2.99
Alphabet	1-57768-151-7	$2.99
Division	1-57768-158-4	$2.99
Money	1-57768-150-9	$2.99
Multiplication	1-57768-157-6	$2.99
Numbers	1-57768-127-4	$2.99
Phonics	1-57768-152-5	$2.99
Sight Words	1-57768-160-6	$2.99
Subtraction	1-57768-168-1	$2.99
Telling Time	1-57768-138-X	$2.99

Prices subject to change without notice.

FIRST READERS

MERCER MAYER FIRST READERS
SKILLS AND PRACTICE

Levels 1, 2, 3 (Grades PreK–2) • 24 Pages • Size: 6" x 9" • Paperback

Young readers will enjoy these simple and engaging stories written with their reading level in mind. Featuring Mercer Mayer's charming illustrations and favorite Little Critter characters, these are the books children will want to read again and again. To ensure reading success, the First Readers are based on McGraw-Hill's respected educational SRA Open Court Reading Program. Skill-based activities in the back of the book also help reinforce learning. A word list is included for vocabulary practice. Each book contains 24 full-color pages.

Level 1 (Grades PreK–K)

TITLE	ISBN	PRICE
Camping Out	1-57768-806-6	$3.95
No One Can Play	1-57768-804-X	$3.95
Play Ball	1-57768-803-1	$3.95
Snow Day	1-57768-805-8	$3.95
Little Critter Slipcase 1	1-57768-823-6	$15.95
(Contains 4 titles; 1 each of the above titles)		
Show and Tell	1-57768-835-X	$3.95
New Kid in Town	1-57768-829-5	$3.95
Country Fair	1-57768-827-9	$3.95
My Trip to the Zoo	1-57768-826-0	$3.95
Little Critter Slipcase 2	1-57768-853-8	$15.95
(Contains 4 titles; 1 each of the above titles)		

Level 2 (Grades K–1)

TITLE	ISBN	PRICE
The Mixed-Up Morning	1-57768-808-2	$3.95
A Yummy Lunch	1-57768-809-0	$3.95
Our Park	1-57768-807-4	$3.95
Field Day	1-57768-813-9	$3.95
Little Critter Slipcase 1	1-57768-824-4	$15.95
(Contains 4 titles; 1 each of the above titles)		
Beach Day	1-57768-844-9	$3.95
The New Fire Truck	1-57768-843-0	$3.95
A Day at Camp	1-57768-836-8	$3.95
Tiger's Birthday	1-57768-828-7	$3.95
Little Critter Slipcase 2	1-57768-854-6	$15.95
(Contains 4 titles; 1 each of the above titles)		

Level 3 (Grades 1–2)

TITLE	ISBN	PRICE
Surprise!	1-57768-814-7	$3.95
Our Friend Sam	1-57768-815-5	$3.95
Helping Mom	1-57768-816-3	$3.95
My Trip to the Farm	1-57768-817-1	$3.95
Little Critter Slipcase 1	1-57768-825-2	$15.95
(Contains 4 titles; 1 each of the above titles)		
Grandma's Garden	1-57768-846-5	$3.95
Class Trip	1-57768-845-7	$3.95
Goodnight, Little Critter	1-57768-834-1	$3.95
Our Tree House	1-57768-833-3	$3.95
Little Critter Slipcase 2	1-57768-855-4	$15.95
(Contains 4 titles; 1 each of the above titles)		

Prices subject to change without notice.

The Children's Book Council has named **Snow Day** and **Our Friend Sam** recipients of the Council's "Children's Choices 2002" awards, placing the two titles among the highest recommended books for children.